GET MOVING
MOTIVATION FOR LIVING

GET MOVING

MOTIVATION FOR LIVING

Paul White

CF4·K

10 9 8 7 6 5 4 3 2 1

Get Moving ISBN 978-1-84550-629-2

© Copyright 1976 Paul White

First published by Anzea Books 1976

Reprinted 1977, 1981, 1983

Also published by the Paternoster Press by agreement
with Anzea

Published in 2011 by Christian Focus Publications,
Geanies House, Fearn, Tain, Ross-shire, IV20 1TW,
Scotland, U.K.

Cover design: Daniel van Straaten

Cover photo: Istockphoto

Interior illustrations: Graham Wade

Printed and bound by Norhaven, Denmark

CONTENTS

Fact File: Paul White

Born in 1910 in Bowral, New South Wales, Australia, Paul had Africa in his blood for as long as he could remember. His father captured his imagination with stories of his experiences in the Boer War which left an indelible impression. His father died of meningitis in army camp in 1915, and he was left an only child without his father at five years of age. He inherited his father's storytelling gift along with a mischievous sense of humour.

He committed his life to Christ as a sixteen-year-old schoolboy and studied medicine as the next step towards missionary work in Africa. Paul and his wife, Mary, left Sydney, with their small son, David, for Tanganyika in 1938. He always thought of this as his life's work but Mary's severe illness forced their early return to Sydney in 1941. Their daughter, Rosemary, was born while they were overseas.

Within weeks of landing in Sydney Paul was invited to begin a weekly radio broadcast which spread throughout Australia as the Jungle Doctor Broadcasts - the last of these was aired in 1985. The weekly scripts for these programmes became the raw material for the Jungle Doctor hospital stories - a series of twenty books.

Paul always said he preferred life to be a 'mixed grill' and so it was: writing, working as a rheumatologist, public speaking, involvement with many Christian organisations, adapting the fable stories into multiple forms (comic books, audio cassettes, filmstrips), radio and television, and sharing his love of birds with others by producing bird song cassettes - and much more.

The books in part or whole have been translated into 109 languages.

Paul saw that although his plan to work in Africa for life was turned on its head, in God's better planning he was able to reach more people by coming home than by staying. It was a great joy to meet people over the years who told him they were on their way overseas to work in mission because of the books.

Paul's wife, Mary, died after a long illness in 1970. He married Ruth and they had the joy of working together on many new projects. He died in 1992 but the stories and fables continue to attract an enthusiastic readership of all ages.

Stethescopes, the thorn trees of Tanzania, adventures of an ancient model Ford, life-or-death surgery by flickering lamplight, monkeys and giraffes, vultures and crocodiles - in story after riveting story; here is a book to captivate readers of every age, and of every country.

Paul White, 'The Jungle Doctor,' has become known by his books across all five continents, and in scores of languages. Get Moving is a kind of modern Pilgrim's Progress, in its portrayal – drawn from the thrills and spills of fifty years - of the Christian life. The whole sweep of it all is found in thirty chunky chapters; the start, the up-turns, the challenges, the power-source. Doubts? Guidance? Our Christian confidence? Prayer and the Bible? Marriage and sex? Ambition? Money? Witness? The Jungle Doctor has motored his way through the entire turrain.

Enjoy the book, a chapter a night – for a month! Get Moving makes an attractive and life-forming gift, to anyone embarking on discipleship – and those of us who could do with a refreshing review and uplift.

Richard Bewes O.B.E.
West London

1
TASTE OF EXPLOSIVES
Dynamite!

The old African man sneered.

'You say that stuff, which looks like sand mixed with the fat of a goat can split this?'

He spat forcibly and accurately at a grey rock the size of four elephants.

'The words are true, Great One,' said Daudi, one of the key men in the jungle hospital.

'The words are hollow, empty and entirely foolish,' scoffed the old man.

I smiled. 'Let us prove to you that this is not the case. To do so is not a difficult matter. Be here an hour before sunset and see for yourself.'

Daudi nodded. 'This will bring the whole thing to your understanding, Great One. They will drill a hole as deep as from the tips of your fingers to your elbow and as thick as a corn stalk.'

'Into this they place carefully this stuff called dynamite,' I broke in. 'And see, these wires will be pushed into it. They run to this heavy thing we call a battery. This is the handle that when you push...'

There was disgust in his voice. 'Words and words. It is beyond common sense to think that boxes and wires and that goat's fat stuff have power.' He stalked away.

But in the late afternoon, he and a hundred others were back.

Questions and comments came from all directions:

'What is this substance of power?'

'Do you think this stuff will do what he says?'

'The Bwana Doctor seems to have faith in it.'

'It is called dynamite. It has great power.'

The loud-voiced old man laughed. 'Come and watch this thing of small wisdom. Join your laughter with mine when he drops his medicine so carefully into the hole they have made and fiddles with his wires and his heavy, black box. And then, at his word, the rock will be torn apart.' He made elaborate hand movements. His voice was loaded with scorn.

I smiled. 'You describe it well, Great One. Also there will be a noise like thunder; and pieces of stone, small and large will fly in all directions.'

An African schoolboy said quietly, 'That is what happens indeed. I have read about it.'

'Shut your ignorant mouth,' roared the old man.

I turned to all the people. 'I shall count to twenty slowly. Shelter behind strong trees and boulders or, if you prefer it, crouch down in holes. There is small joy in being injured by flying rock.'

There was a general scramble for safety except for the old man who stood legs wide apart, arms on his hips, scornfully watching.

Everything was checked and rechecked.

Crouched behind a substantial tree, I counted. When I reached fifteen I shouted, 'Lie on the ground, Great One. There is danger!'

'*Kah!* I have no fear.'

I called out to the people: 'We have warned him; should anything happen to him, it is his own affair.'

I went on counting, '… nineteen, twenty.'

Down went the handle.

There was a loud explosion.

The rock split apart. A wedge of stone as big as his head whizzed past the old man. With a gasp he threw himself to the ground, his hands over his ears. When there was no further explosion he leapt to his feet and disappeared into the thorn bush at surprising speed.

Daudi slapped his thigh and laughed till tears came into his eyes. He turned to the excited watchers holding up two fingers. 'Because you don't understand things and haven't yet seen them, that doesn't mean they can't happen. That doesn't mean they don't have great power.'

'Truly it is the way with dynamite,' came a voice.

'It is also the way with God,' said my African friend.

He was right. When God comes into a person's life, he makes a vast difference to that life and the way it is lived. He brings purpose and power to our existence here and now.

It becomes clear that this is the beginning of something infinitely greater. We become individual, active parts of God's tremendous plan for men.

God's way has been dynamite in my life.

The stone we cracked that day later was used in building a hospital. That hospital was a means of easing considerable suffering and saving many lives.

God's way gives the foundation for life, the building material for character, the motivation for outreach and action, and, as a bonus, deep satisfaction.

2
LIGHTING THE FUSE
Conversion

'You're a liar,' said the old carpenter softly. 'I saw you hit that hen with a stone from your catapult.'

He had heard me tell an elaborate story of how the elderly bird had fallen from its perch and broken its leg.

I knew I was a liar and I was well aware that there was a collection of other things that I had done or not done which left me out on a limb as far as God was concerned.

I was an acutely uncomfortable ten-year-old. I had read and remembered words from almost the last page of the Bible. They left no doubt as to God's view of the matter.

The words were about heaven. 'But nothing unclean, no one who deals in filthiness and lies, shall ever at any time enter it—but only those whose names are written in the Lamb's book of life' (Revelation 21:27 Phillips).

What I badly wanted to know was how my name could be written in that book.

This was something I did not find easy to talk about. Only twice did I ask for help. On each occasion I chose the most inopportune time. Once I was snubbed by a minister; and the second time, my mother, who was cooking Saturday's dinner, told me to ask later on.

I never did.

For years my conscience throbbed with the knowledge that there was something radically wrong. I was well aware that my soul was sick. I knew about the cure. But knowing about the cure was as unhelpful as having the medicine but not knowing exactly how to get it into my system. The answer became clear when my seventeenth birthday was in sight.

One hot night in a large tent, a very straight-talking Irishman, W. P. Nicholson, hit me hard. He was very clear and direct.

'Your back is turned to God. You're doing what you know to be wrong and not doing the things you know to be right. You're in trouble because nothing you can do will help you out of a deadly situation. It's by grace—a gift you don't deserve—that you'll find your only way out. What you do—your achievements—are in no way the answer.'

He quoted, 'How shall we escape if we ignore such a great salvation?' (Hebrews 2:3)

He spelled out the steps to be taken.

A—Admit that you're a sinner. This is what the Bible says in the first epistle that John wrote: 'But if we freely admit that we have sinned, we find God utterly reliable and straightforward—He forgives our sins and makes us thoroughly clean from all that is evil' (1 John 1:9 Phillips).

B—Believe in the Lord Jesus Christ. 'Yet to all who received him, to those who believed in his name, he gave the right to become children of God' (John 1:12). Now to become a child of God two things are necessary. There is something to be believed. There is Someone to be received.

C—Commit your life into his hands. You hand him the title deeds of your life. You ask him to come right into your life to be your Lord.

The actual words I used were, 'Please God, forgive me for my sins. Give me everlasting life and show me what you want me to do with my life here on earth.'

After I had prayed this prayer, I got up from my knees and fiddled for an hour with a 1926 model radio set, with valves as big as light globes and a loud speaker that looked like the outgoing end of a French horn.

Neither that night nor the days that followed did anything unusual happen. There were no cloud-top experiences, no special feelings, no exotic sense of change. It was all rather flat.

But it was a beginning.

I was reluctant to talk about it. Perhaps I'd be laughed at or be considered ignorant. I hung on with my mind in a whirl.

It was my habit to run a brisk mile round the local streets between the end of my school homework and bedtime.

A rather useful time to think.

I realised that putting my life into Jesus Christ's hands involved a complete round-about-turn for mind, feet, and behaviour, for which the technical word is repentance.

It became clear that he wanted to hold the wheel of my life and do the steering.

3

BLASTING DOUBTS
The Resurrection

Doubts by the bagful started to hit me. It was disturbing to be bruised by questions raised by those who had little or no time for the new way that I had chosen.

This was not eased by those I asked to help me. Some people used words with which I was unfamiliar or lost me in technicalities. Others seemed to turn on a recording. Others still were vague or didn't know the answers. What astounded me was that some seemed to feel that this vagueness showed the quality of their faith.

I talked to my science master—an untidy, very knowledgeable man who delighted to talk about oriental poetry, Buddhism or orchids, in the middle of a chemistry class. He could be trusted to take seriously anything you had to say.

During a practical class I told him that I had asked Jesus to run my life. He looked at me in a rather pained way and said, 'Go for facts, White. That all sounds rather emotional.' He turned down a Bunsen burner and went on, 'There is some evidence that Jesus of Nazareth existed. He is mentioned by Josephus and elsewhere. There is a tradition that he died on a cross and there is the story of what is called the resurrection. But in anyone's thinking an empty tomb is a remarkably poor foundation for a religion. Now get on with your work.'

Help came from a square-chinned lawyer.

His professional interest had been stirred as he had read the reports of the resurrection in the book of Acts. He had thought deeply and was able to express himself in a crisp, understandable way that made the matter very clear to me. Wisely he didn't overwhelm me with his ideas. Rather he stimulated my appetite to find out for myself.

He smiled and said, 'Read what the Bible has to say, and have a solid look at the evidence. I'm available if you want to talk about the whole thing later. Why not look at the people and places and events involved? You'll find it's an eye-opener.'

This started me off reading the Bible with a purpose, with a pencil in my hand.

I read carefully about Jesus' birth, and saw that Christmas was not the critical day. His conception was unique. His birth was certainly dramatic. It was marked by a vision of angels, a visitation of wise men and unusual astronomy and publicity that brought about political multi-murder of infants.

Jesus escaped.

He grew into a wonderful teacher, preacher, leader and healer. And he died.

All this and he could have still been mere man. A wonderful man but nothing more. Then came the proving time when he was thirty-three.

At the peak of his ministry everything seemed to crash. His utterly unusual activity was forgotten by the vast majority. Cheering changed to clamour for his death. And die he did—a wretched death, nailed agonisingly to a cross, flanked by criminals. If he had died like anybody else and been buried that would have been the end of the chapter.

It wasn't.

Listen to the people who were there and saw it happen.

There was the Roman centurion, a tough soldier, who seeing Jesus die muttered, 'Surely he was the Son of God!' (Matthew 27:54)

There was Peter who behaved like a coward during Jesus' trial but, in a matter of days after seeing Jesus alive, was prepared to face prison and death to tell what he knew.

Thomas, the blunt, fact-demanding man; the won't-believe-it-till-I-touch-it Thomas. This man changed suddenly from miserable doubt to belief. He met Jesus. He didn't even need to touch him. He said, 'My Lord and my God!' (John 20:28)

Evidence continued to pile up.

Mary Magdalene's sight was blurred by weeping but she recognised Jesus' voice.

The disciples as a group saw him, spoke with him and ate with him.

Five hundred people saw Jesus at one time.

Later Saul of Tarsus, when he saw Jesus face to face, did a complete about-turn, changing from a zealous enemy to one of God's greatest champions. Later on he wrote, 'The rising of Christ from the dead is the very heart of our message' (1 Corinthians 15:12 Phillips).

He had had the chance of talking to the people who had seen the happenings. He'd heard their talk, noticed their sincerity and the minute details of their observation. He had seen the almost startling change that had occurred in their lives.

The parcel of words that Paul had written hit me. I had read them and heard them read frequently. They are in the burial service. But on this reading a powerful light seemed to be turned on in my understanding. 'And if Christ was not raised then neither our preaching nor your faith has any meaning at all … and if Christ did not rise your faith is futile and your sins have never been forgiven … Truly, if our hope in Christ were limited to this life only we should, of all mankind, be the most to be pitied! But the glorious fact is that Christ did rise from the dead' (1 Corinthians 15:14, 17, 19-20 Phillips).

Jesus, whom I had asked to be my rescuer and my leader, is God. He is alive. I am not serving a dead adviser but a living Lord. I was gripped by the thought of what a dynamic thing it is to have a living, on-the-spot, always in touch with me Lord who wanted to see my life have drive, purpose and results. He is here to show me the way and to lift me when I crash.

The empty grave was not the result of zealous body-snatching by disciples with an obsession, but a place for which the crucified Son of God had no further use. He had overcome death.

And thinking of the cross, the fact that the resurrection occurred lifts the Lord's death far above any mere martyr's death.

It was God's planned way of showing his supreme love to mankind. It was prophesied in numerous places, especially Isaiah chapter 53, pictured in the Jewish sacrifices of the Old Testament, and foreshadowed in a different way in such incidents as Isaac's escape in Genesis chapter 22. Psalm 22 gives a vivid account of the Crucifixion in poetic form. The cross did what no person can do for himself or herself. Jesus himself, innocent and without a trace of sin, faced the tremendous ordeal not only of pain, agony and shame but the much greater one of personally carrying the sin of everyone. This cut him off from God. We, who through our sinning are blocked off from God, suddenly find ourselves able to face him without guilt and blame. Jesus took the punishment and, living, he is our link with God the Father today. 'As his personal representatives we say, "Make your peace with God". For God caused Christ, who himself knew nothing of sin, actually to be sin for our sakes, so that in Christ we might be made good with the goodness of God' (2 Corinthians 5:20-21 Phillips).

I was dealing with the supernatural. I realised that a tremendous change must have occurred in me, if I really believed what God said. I had become a new creature.

I had entered the early, less important stage of eternal life. The body stage.

Death had had its teeth drawn as far as I was concerned.

Life had a purpose. Jesus himself had stated it. 'I came to bring them life, and far more life than before. I am the good Shepherd' (John 10:10 Phillips).

Jesus Christ is my Shepherd and my Lord; I am under his orders.

Not wandering in unplanned activity.

Not stumbling along thinking wishfully.

The Holy Spirit was working on my mind and spirit.

Through him the Bible became alive and I had open communication to God.

I was really on to something tremendous. It was dynamite!

4
MAKE A U-TURN
Repentance

Repentance was the first subject on which Jesus spoke.

John the Baptist struck the same note forcibly—Repent.

Peter's first sermon had the punch line, 'Repent, then, and turn to God, so that your sins may be wiped out' (Acts 3:19).

Put this word under the microscope, look at it, see it clearly, focus tightly and avoid all vagueness.

Repentance is the gateway into God's new life. It is a complete change of mind. When you repent, you turn from sin to God, you go his way and do his will.

It's revolutionary. Your thinking, your attitudes, your outlook is changed from the roots up. The change of mind involves hating sin and loving God with all your heart.

Let me picture repentance for you African fashion.

Small monkey had been walloped on his hairless portion with the flat of his uncle's great jungle knife.

His eyes gleamed as he saw his elderly relation stroll off through the jungle. Nimbly he climbed the family tree, his tail wrapped round the knife's handle. Out he went on his uncle's favourite limb and peered into the deep dark ravine below him, 'Won't he be furious,' chuckled little monkey, 'when this limb goes down there.'

He started chopping.

Chips flew.

Giraffe looked up at him, 'Monkey, change your mind about what you're doing and change your mind about where you're standing.'

But little monkey had eyes only for the cutting edge of the knife and the chips that flew from the limb.

'Change your mind, change your direction. Can't you see what will happen?' shouted giraffe.

Monkey chortled and swished the knife at his long-necked friend. He took no notice and chopped on with enthusiasm.

His monkey intelligence did not tell him what it meant to be out on a limb, over a gulch and on the wrong side of the chop.

'Change your mind, change your direction,' yelled giraffe.

The limb creaked and monkey muscle bulged.

Chop.

The limb cracked. Monkey swung the knife in the air, 'It won't be long now.'

It wasn't.

Chop.

The limb broke. Monkey, knife, limb and all went down, down, down...

Unlike monkey, you will have realised the meaning of repentance and its importance. To repent opens up a new life. Not to repent is mere monkey wisdom.

Repentance is not merely to interrupt a habit.

It is not a New Year resolution or a change of living during Lent.

It is not merely being sorry you were found out.

That is remorse, an uncomfortable and comparatively useless state.

Repentance is being sorry enough not to do it again.

Repentance is an action for keeps.

This doesn't mean that you won't or can't fall or stumble. It does mean however that even though you are stumbling or perhaps groping your way, it is in the new direction along God's way.

Don't forget his strength is available to help you. God's book says: 'I can do everything through him who gives me strength' (Philippians 4:13). This is a cheque you can cash on God's bank.

Change of mind leads to change of person.

This is known as being a *new creature* or the *new birth*. Have a look at 2 Corinthians 5, verse 17: 'For if a man is in Christ he becomes a new person altogether—the past is finished and gone, everything has become fresh and new' (Phillips).

Look also at 1 Peter 1, verse 3 and a few verses on: 'We men have been born again into a life full of hope, through Christ's rising again from the dead! You can now hope for a perfect inheritance beyond the reach of change and decay, "reserved" in heaven for you. And in the meantime you are guarded by the power of God operating through your faith' (Phillips).

5
NEGOTIATING POTHOLES
Assurance

One of my ambitions was to succeed in athletics. Middle distance running was my area.

What I needed was a top-quality coach.

I found one. Was he competent! And was he tough!!

'You want to win, Paul? Right! You must be completely fit and properly motivated. Now listen carefully. Your diet. Out go meat pies, cakes, sweets, pastry … got it?'

I had.

'Concentrate on protein. You mustn't carry an ounce of useless weight. To bed at 10 p.m. Eight hours' sleep EVERY NIGHT. Got it?'

I nodded again.

'You don't smoke or drink? Good. You'd better not. As for training, here's a schedule:

'Run at least five miles a day for a month to tone up your muscles. Then we'll get down to real hard work. You need to build muscle, stamina, guts, the will to win...'

Next he ordered a close-fitting knapsack containing two house bricks. Wearing this on my back I ran over sand hills.

It was hard, exhausting and almost unbearable but great stuff when it came to the big race.

The way I chose to live my life went uphill and continues to do so. Jesus makes it clear both from how he lived and from what he said, that the path ahead of those who put themselves into his hands would not be smooth. It's uphill, often steeply so. He doesn't undertake to move the obstacles out of the way.

He says the going will be rough and the path narrow. It will be set about with all manner of adventures, which include danger, buffeting and bruises.

Jesus doesn't undertake to give you immunity from difficulties. But he does offer strength and the weapons to deal with the real opposition. Satan, the enemy of man's soul, takes very little interest in you as long as you are going his way of meandering along a neutral path. You are doing nothing to upset his plans. But the moment you turn and go God's way, Satan sets to work, although not necessarily throwing everything at you at the beginning. He's a very skilled performer indeed and has a fine collection of tricks.

Early in the piece, I suddenly seemed to stumble into a hailstorm of problems:

Were my sins forgiven? Could I be *sure* they were forgiven? Was it all a sort of a daydream?

Had my prayers been mere words, stopping short at the ceiling?

How was I to know?

I was in no small turmoil. Again, as I had been advised, I turned to the Bible. There was the place where Jesus himself said, 'I solemnly assure you that the man who hears what I have to say and believes in the One who has sent Me has eternal life. He does not have to face judgment, he has already passed from death into life' (John 5:24 Phillips).

That sounded clear cut. Was there any good reason why I shouldn't believe him? Again he said, 'My sheep listen to my voice; I know them, and they follow me. I give them eternal life, and they shall never perish; no one can snatch them out of my hand' (John 10: 27, 28). There it was. I had joined his flock and I was doing my best to listen to his voice. Why should I doubt?

About this time an aunt of mine sent me a cheque for five pounds.[1] It had my name written on it and her signature was on the bottom. She had also carefully inscribed the cheque so that nobody could cash it but myself. I looked it over two or three times to be sure that all was well. I had no particular reason to believe that my aunt would tantalise me with a useless piece of paper. After all I was one of the family.

---

1. Because of inflation a cheque for £5 or $5 would have been worth quite a bit more than it is today.

I took that cheque to the bank, endorsed it in the required way and put it down on the counter in front of the teller. He looked at it, ticked it with his pencil, checked that I had written my signature on the back and said in a matter-of-fact voice, 'How would you like it?'

'In ten shilling notes,' I replied and walked, smiling, out of the bank with the money in my pocket.

Outside the door I stopped. If I was prepared to have faith in my aunt and her signature in the matter of a cheque and five pounds, why shouldn't I have confidence in Almighty God, for this life and the next?

If God was all-powerful why shouldn't I take him at his word?

It was like turning on a light.

That light has burnt on all through my life.

Jesus often used stories to make his points clear.

As a medical missionary in Africa I learnt to do the same thing.

I didn't *feel* different. This monkey story has helped me to resolve the problem of feelings.

Little monkey had a consuming desire to cross the equator. He thought it would feel wonderful to be in the northern hemisphere. So he scampered through the treetops. There was a gap where the road cut through the jungle. On this road were a broad yellow line and a signpost pointing in two directions. One read Northern Hemisphere and the other, Southern Hemisphere. Being an educated monkey he knew where he was. He climbed out on a limb. Without doubt he was sitting in the Southern Hemisphere. He spent quite a time thinking how wonderful it would be in the North. He was all worked up about it. There were tinglings in his tail and pins and needles in other portions of his monkey anatomy. His eyes sparkled.

He licked his lips and sprang.

Directly below him was the yellow line. Then he was beyond it and clinging to the limb of another tree. He could see the signpost saying Northern Hemisphere. He was there!

He sat for a long time on that limb. His tingling and pins and needles disappeared. His enthusiasm drained away. He was still the same monkey. He felt no different.

Giraffe, who was his particular adviser, said, 'Listen, monkey, you have to face facts. Geography is geography. There's the signpost showing you where you are. Stay sitting where you are and thinking as you are and you'll keep on not feeling any different. Just crossing the line is not enough. Get moving! The further you travel north the surer you'll be that you've crossed the line.'

This is how it worked out for me. I was on God's side. I kept on travelling. I understood that the prayer, 'Hold up my goings in your path,' did not mean, 'Hold up my sittings on your path.'

Things started to happen and I realised whose side I was on and where I was going. It's a tremendous help to get the facts in focus and keep them there.

I had invited the Lord Jesus Christ to forgive me, to make me one of his family and to take control of my life.

To experience the change, I needed to travel on— on God's terms, going his way. To do this, God's book needed to come off the shelf and to be built into my everyday living.

6
OFFICIAL TRAVEL GUIDE
Authority

My athletics coach looked me squarely in the face. That afternoon I had been beaten by men who previously had been comfortably accounted for. What made it worse was that the time for the race was slow although there was little wind and the track was good.

The coach's voice was very firm, 'Listen, Paul, you took that beating for one reason only: you didn't follow my rules.'

He moved a step closer and gripped my shoulders. 'Remember. I call the tune not you.'

I had relaxed a bit with cream cake, lemon meringue pies and my favourite—chocolate. I was a trifle overweight and underwinded.

My coach was aware of it the moment I stepped on to the track. My teammates knew half way through the race and I'd known it for two weeks before.

After that there was no doubt in my mind as to what I should do if I wanted athletic success.

In the wider field of life, however, it was not so clear.

Irishmen have had a considerable effect on my life. I've told you about W. P. Nicholson and how he put me spiritually into gear. It was then I felt the pinch of uphill travel. I was going God's way under his command, but it wasn't easy.

As a first-year undergraduate I came up against the rough surf of university life.

What was to be my attitude to a score of things?

'Be broad-minded, man,' urged some. They took a very different approach to many things that I had regarded as being over the boundary as far as I was concerned.

I looked questioningly to some Christian people I really respected. They would be horrified at the mention of a lot of things that I didn't see as particularly vicious—like reading whodunits and going to the pictures occasionally when I'd checked up on the content of the show.

Other things frowned upon were topless bathing costumes (for boys), the pack of playing cards with which I did conjuring tricks—even football!

What were the guidelines to a Christian's living?

At this stage I met my second Irishman. He was just through his medical course and in his mid-twenties. He answered my questions and stirred my imagination. He brought to myself and to scores of other students in Canada, New Zealand and Australia what they both wanted and needed.

He put things pithily.

'Becoming a Christian is not like joining a club or taking on a spare-time job. Jesus rescues you when you are in a hopeless state, whether you realise it or not. He says very plainly, "If anyone would come after me, he must deny himself and take up his cross daily and follow me" (Luke 9:23).

'He gives the orders. You obey.

'He is the authority. What he says goes.

'He asks for complete authority over your life: your time, your ambitions, your friends, your music, your skills, your sport—the lot.'

I can still hear the voices raised in protest. 'Hold it. That's only your opinion.'

'It is not,' said Howard Guinness. 'It's God's clear statement. The Bible, God's written Word, is your guideline with clear-cut pointers on which way to go and which way not to go in every circumstance. It's your supreme authority in all matters, whether in belief or behaviour.'

He was right. I have found this to be the truth.

God makes his orders come into our thinking and our understanding through his Word. Our obvious responsibility is to read it, think about it and memorise it.

The Bible states principles from a number of angles. They are clear and easily understood. But not so easily obeyed. This is where the Holy Spirit comes in.

Our responsibility is to fill our minds and memories with the counsel of God. The Holy Spirit impresses on our consciousness the particular part of that counsel which applies to any problem, event or cross-road in our living.

The Lord Jesus Christ, when you ask him to take charge of your life, will do so on his terms. He must be in charge. He gives the orders. He expects obedience to those orders. Not selective obedience, doing only what suits your tastes, convenience and opinions. Don't take a pair of scissors to the Bible.

I like the crisp way in which Jesus said, 'If you love me, you will obey what I command' (John 14.15).

And the words from the first letter of John chapter 2, verse 3: 'It is only when we obey God's laws that we can be quite sure that we really know him. The man who claims to know God but does not obey his laws is not only a liar but lives in self-delusion' (Phillips).

Sharp, stark focus that.

7
GUIDEBOOK
Bible Reading

The first day I worked in hospital as a doctor, the medical superintendent said, 'You're starting out in medical practice today. Here is a small book listing the tried and trusted medicines available from the dispensary here. These are the results of careful observation of many experienced physicians and surgeons. Get this book into your head and use its contents in your daily routine.'

The obvious thing was to memorise the lot.

My routine was to listen to the patient's story, examine him and prescribe. The medicine given was not a concoction thought up on the spur of the moment, but a proven effective remedy from the standard book. This is what my planned approach was in the day-to-day detail of my profession.

In the broad sweep of my life the same thing was true. As a Christian I have a practical handbook for living—the Bible.

I use it daily.

Its practical usefulness is tremendous.

It has been so for millions of people for hundreds of years.

The small hospital pharmacopoeia on the other hand is almost a museum piece after some quarter of a century.

As you talk these things over with your friends you will frequently hear that nothing is *right* or *wrong*, *true* or *false*—it all depends on your point of view.

But does it? The Bible makes it clear that it is God's viewpoint that matters.

This does not change from century to century or from year to year. Man's viewpoint alters dizzily and disconcertingly. God's viewpoint is solid rock—a firm path you can tread safely, whatever is going on around you.

If the Bible says 'don't,' you have the stop sign right in front of you. There is no debate.

You can follow with confidence the clear statement of God's book, 'All scripture is inspired by God and is useful for teaching the faith and correcting error, for resetting the direction of a man's life and training him in good living. The scriptures are the comprehensive equipment of the man of God, and fit him fully for all branches of his work' (2 Timothy 3: 16,17 Phillips).

The Bible tells us what to believe and how to behave. It isn't a charm to bring you good luck or an idol to be gazed at reverently, carefully wrapped in plastic or placed behind glass.

You don't consult it from time to time like an encyclopedia.

It is useless to feel things will go better if you merely have a Bible on your bookshelf or bedside table.

Unread, it's as helpful to you as a life-saving medicine left on the shelf or worn around the neck on a gold chain.

The old African man was full of misery. 'My head,' he groaned. 'My neck, my shoulders, they ache. They fill me with no joy … Oh, my back.'

He slumped down on a stool, put his face in his hands and minutely described his pain and all the other bad news.

Fortunately the treatment was simple and would be most effective. 'Grandfather, take courage and swallow two of these pills at sunup, two more at midday and at sunset two more. Understand?'

He nodded his head and groaned as he did so.

For safety, I went over it again. 'That is two, three times a day.' Again he grunted.

'Now are you sure you understand how to take this medicine?'

'Am I a fool?' he hissed...

Two weeks later he was back, no better and full of complaints. 'The medicine had no strength; I am no better. Pain still fills my bones and my body.'

'Grandfather, did you take this medicine as we told you?'

A cunning look spread over his face. 'To have swallowed them would have been to waste them.'

He undid the cloth that was wound round his body. A piece of string was round his neck and dangling at the level of his heart was a parcel of banana bark. He undid this. Inside were the pills.

'My way of wisdom is to hold this medicine against my head when it aches. To hold it against my shoulders when they ache, to put it over my back, my legs, my knees, my ankles.' He spat, 'But it is a medicine of no strength.'

He was amazed an hour later at the way his pain had diminished when he swallowed two of the white pills.

God's book is full of power and intense practical usefulness. If you haven't found it so to date, perhaps you are following the same technique as the old African.

In the matter of pills it is not enough to have them or to be close to them. They need to be inside you, to be part of you, to deal with your particular need. You need to take them regularly, then you find they work. In this way your troubles and discomforts are dealt with and you have strength to live satisfyingly.

The more you build God's book into your memory and weave it into the pattern of your behaviour, the more readily can the Holy Spirit show you God's way. Along a similar line, food in the pantry does very much less for you than a meal in the stomach.

Reading God's book is not merely a useful, rewarding thing to do. It's vital for growth.

'I have treasured the words of his mouth more than my daily bread' (Job 23: 12).

Reading the Bible should be no haphazard business.

Poking your finger into the book and reading a few verses will get you nowhere. Remember the unfortunate man who when asked did he appreciate the dictionary said, 'Yes, very much, but I found it a bit hard to get the thread of the story.' You need a system, a plan, to read God's word. It is when you follow this through that you're in a position to be guided by the Spirit of God as you read.

You follow the routine of so many meals a day and occasional snacks and drinks to keep your body on the move. Why not do the same sort of thing for your spirit to ensure its growth? It needs to be nourished.

Follow a system in putting muscle round your soul. I have found the one that Scripture Union works out is very valuable and the notes that they produce help to explain background and theological points that my own reading and education have not covered. Read God's book daily and you'll find a benefit in a class with dynamite. Problems your hands cannot deal with are readily torn apart by the power of God.

'But the man who looks into the perfect mirror of God's law, the law of liberty, and makes a habit of so doing, is not the man who sees and forgets. He puts that law into practice and he wins true happiness' (James 1:25 Phillips).

This is the system drawn up by Scripture Union:

PRAY before reading that God will help you to understand what you read. Psalm 119:18: 'Open my eyes, that I may see wonderful things in your law.'

READ carefully through the Bible passage, looking for God's message to you.

THINK about what you have read, and seek to answer some of these questions:

a. What does this Bible passage teach about God— the Father, his Son Jesus Christ, or the Holy Spirit?

b. What does it teach about life? Is there a command, a promise, or a warning? Is there an example to follow, or a sin to avoid?

c. What is the main lesson?

WRITE down any verse or thought you have found helpful.

PRAY, using the thoughts you have gained as a basis for your prayer.

MEMORISE a verse each week.

8
COMMUNICATIONS
Prayer

You don't need to understand electricity to throw a switch to warm yourself, to have light or music, or to cook your food.

You don't have to understand everything about Almighty God to talk to him.

I arrived in East Africa a year or so before Hitler's war and bought at bargain price a shortwave valve radio. The people who came to our jungle hospital at that time had never seen a radio set. They had little or no idea how it worked or what it could do.

I had heard that the BBC would that day broadcast for the first time in Swahili, the local language.

An eager and excited crowd turned up and noisily discussed what was about to happen. I listened to various voices.

'It's all lies. No voice can come out of that box. It's too small to have even a child hidden inside it.'

'It is a thing of wonder.'

'It's not a thing of commonsense.'

There was a chuckle, 'He will have shame when the time comes and nothing happens.'

'Perhaps,' came a scared whisper, 'perhaps it's a box full of witchcraft.'

'Listen everybody.' I made myself heard above the noise. 'This is a machine very well known in my country. It makes it possible for you to hear the voice of someone very far away. The one who will be speaking in a few moments is speaking to you from England.'

Again there was a doubtful murmur. 'How does it work?' came a loud voice.

'I push this button, twist this knob and turn that one.' I proceeded to tune in.

Shrill noises came from the antiquated valve set. Some of my audience bolted. Others looked scared but stood their ground. However everyone relaxed when clear and loud came a warm voice.

'*Jambo, watu wote*. Good day, everybody.'

Every lip moved in the reply. '*Jambo Bwana*. Good day, sir.'

The voice spoke on. The Africans were amazed that such an unlikely thing could happen, but delighted nevertheless.

Of course these days radio is commonplace. The mobile phone and the internet have brought world-wide communication on in leaps and bounds.

Prayer is one of the two great ways of finding God's love and knowing him better. God shapes your life as you pray.

Prayer should be an everyday experience to those who are in God's family.

It is to the soul what breathing is to the body.

It may not make sense to those who have not become Christians. But to those who have, it's a direct line to God.

It's never engaged, never out of order at his end.

To me it's the most important line of communication in my life.

Open Line

There is one call that everybody has a right to make, knowing that God will certainly answer. It is, 'Please God, forgive me.' If you mean it, he answers fully.

If you are not a member of God's family and you live your life with your back turned towards him, you have no reason to expect him to do what you ask in other matters. You have no claim on God if you walk with your back to him and shout for help over your shoulder.

Daily Prayer

If you have become a Christian, don't regard God as a mere convenience, 'Dial-if-in-trouble.' When you

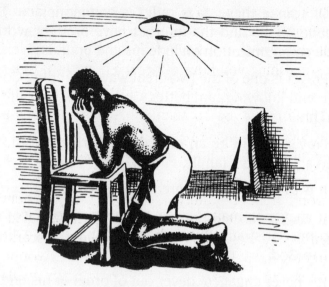

pray do not approach God with, as it were, a shopping list in your hand. Prayer is not a convenient way of getting something out of God. A person *wants* to pray because he loves God.

God has promised to supply all our needs—not our wants. So pray for your needs by all means but don't rush them into first place in your prayer time.

It is important to say 'Good Morning' to God. Having a clean soul is more important than having a clean body. Asking for forgiveness is a daily need.

John puts it this way, 'But if we freely admit that we have sinned, we find God utterly reliable and straight-forward—He forgives our sins and makes us thoroughly clean from all that is evil' (1 John 1:9 Phillips). That's the way to start your praying for the day.

It is never easy and seldom agreeable to admit that you have made a mistake, to apologise for something that you should not have done or to ask forgiveness for something you have done. It's important that you tell God you're sorry. It's logical to ask him to forgive.

This brings you to thanking him for his care in your life. Think for a while of all that it means to be a member of his family. Think how this affects your present and future living.

Don't ponder guiltily over your past. Remember that he has blotted out your sins. He has healed the wounds; there is no cause at all to finger the scars. It's better to look at the Healer than to relive the wounding and healing. It was Jesus himself who made available to us the double cure for our sinning, dealing both with our guilt and sin's power in our lives.

Don't take it as a right. It calls for our deepest thanks.

When you pray and read his book and meditate, he opens up new scope for your living. You see his plans for you in clearer detail.

He gives you a purpose, an objective, a responsibility.

It's stimulating.

It's positive.

Worship is telling God that you love him and that you're more than thankful that he loves you.

At this stage start asking God to show you where to go and how to deal with each circumstance as it arises.

Praying with System

There is great value in having system in your praying both private and with others. I have a book, which gives space for listing those whom I wish to pray for:

Daily.

Weekly.

Monthly.

Also Special Subjects

You may find a fit-in-your-pocket size, loose-leaf notebook very useful in this matter.

The DAILY section. This is in two parts. I list some people in the morning, some in the evening. These are those who are very close to me, or those with sudden special needs.

The ONCE A WEEK pages. On each day of the week I pick a different topic to pray for and I pray about that topic on that day every week. Here I pray for friends, relations, Christian leaders, organisations that have helped me and in which I am involved and especially my local church.

You can think of a dozen ways to build up your prayer list.

The MONTHLY sheets. On each day of the month I pray for a country and the special contacts that I have there. Also for some special phase or angle of life like parliaments, education, research, social service, church activities, the medical profession, literature, authors, publishers, booksellers, Christian radio and television—a score of things that cross my path, my thinking and my interest.

This book is not only a system but is an aid to concentration. If you rely on your memory alone it's easy for your thoughts to stray and your praying to drag to a stop. There is great value in the old Chinese proverb that 'the weakest ink is better than the strongest memory'. Sometimes it is easier to pray if you add small photographs snipped from groups or from magazine material.

SPECIAL SUBJECTS. I itemise these on the left hand page and keep the right side to record answers. Many people keep careful records of their income and expenditure. It's common sense and normal procedure. Your praying is more important than your money can possibly be.

Praying with Others

This can be a stimulating experience and often is, especially if people want to pray. But how boring group prayer is to those who have no enthusiasm in praying and no purpose in talking to God.

There is no closer link between individuals than the deep satisfaction found in praying together.

Can you pray with the one who could well be your life partner? This is an excellent yardstick to show you how happily you could live together. It indicates the direction of your life.

If prayer does not come readily into the picture, then think twice about becoming engaged. People who love God can love each other much more really and satisfyingly than those who do not.

It's worth remembering that in public prayer you speak to God and not to people. There is the well-known shattering comment, 'That was the most eloquent prayer I have ever heard offered to an audience.'

When you pray as a group at the so-called prayer meeting, remember you are there to pray, not to chat or yarn, or listen to lengthy discourses. It's not a good idea to wait for latecomers. Get straight on with the praying. Go with a mind full of things and people to pray for, not armed with a spleen full of gossip, complaint and negativism.

Jesus has given some readily negotiable checks on the matter of prayer. He said, 'Again I tell you that if two of you on earth agree about anything you ask for,' (the idea is of music—if you harmonise together, make a symphony) 'it will be done for you by my Father in heaven. For where two or three come together in my name, there am I with them' (Matthew 18:19-20).

Read this carefully. It's when the people are gathered together in *his* name. If you're doing God's work, living his way, travelling his path, active in his battle, then this applies. The Lord Jesus Christ is there in the centre of your request or project. You cannot invite him into a substandard activity or some action not in line with his plan.

9
NO ANSWER
Unanswered Prayer

'Does God always answer prayer, Doctor?' asked the medical student.

'Yes, definitely yes. But that doesn't mean I always receive what I asked for.'

We talked for a long time. This is a digest of the conversation. In the family prayer Jesus taught us to pray, he used the words 'Your will be done' (Matthew 6:10).

If our request isn't God's will, the answer will be 'No.'

Personally I've asked for very many things and received this answer.

Jesus once said to Peter, 'You do not realise now what I am doing, but later you will understand' (John 13:7). This is exactly true.

I have now the advantage of hindsight and can, years later, see the strategy of the 'no' which was the better way. The results proved it.

Prayer is like a traffic signal. Sometimes it says GO, sometimes STOP and sometimes the amber light, WAIT.

The Bible puts some spotlights on this situation.

- If I cherished sin in my heart, the Lord would not have listened (Psalm 66:18).

- If anyone turns a deaf ear to the law, even his prayers are detestable (Proverbs 28, verse 9).

- But your iniquities have separated you from your God; your sins have hidden his face from you, so that he will not hear (Isaiah 59:2).

- And if ... any of you does not know how to meet any particular problem he has only to ask God—who gives generously to all men without making them feel foolish or guilty—and he may be quite sure that the necessary wisdom will be given him. But he must ask in sincere faith without secret doubts as to whether he really wants God's help or not (James 1:5 Phillips).

- You don't get what you want because you don't ask God for it. And when you do ask he doesn't give it to you, for you ask in quite the wrong spirit—you only want to satisfy your own desires (James 4:3 Phillips).

'*Mmm*,' said the medical student, 'I shall pray more in the time ahead of me, and I shall think more before I speak.'

10
ON THE HOOF
Prayer by Association

Have you ever tried praying on the hoof? There is much usable time spent in travel, which can be usefully employed praying for people and Christian activities.

Walking to the station, there are the neighbours. In the city and elsewhere there are familiar faces and those I feel impelled to pray for. The train passes places and buildings each with its own associations: churches, schools, friends' houses, banks, insurance companies, radio stations, hospitals. In these are very many people that come into my mind's eye.

There are so many I could not remember to pray for if I had not learned the on-the-hoof idea.

Then there are the advertisements. One is for Anderson's sausages. I have a number of friends with that surname. As the train passes the spot I pray for Ruth and Bill and Lois and Frank. There is a certain undertaker; I pray for many friends who share his name.

Praying on the hoof is a practical antidote for temptation. When you are praying to the Lord Jesus Christ you have the enemy on the wrong foot.

Years ago before going to Africa I asked people to pray for me when they were cleaning their boots. Many still do.

I'm passing on the seed of this idea. You can make it sprout in your own life if it fits into your way of doing things. Your great supernatural, God-given weapon to be used in attack and defence is prayer.

If you develop the habit of prayer you will have more enthusiasm for it because it is so worthwhile.

The closer you get to God the more you come to know him. And the more you are *aware* of him answering.

'The prayer of a righteous man is powerful and effective' (James 5:16).

Stop *saying* your prayers and start talking to God. Prayer is not a reciting of words but talking humbly and quietly to your heavenly Father.

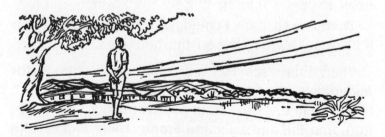

11
GOD'S TELESCOPE
Faith

'You couldn't believe it unless you knew,' said my African friend, looking up from his microscope. 'I thought it was a thing of impossibility when you said there were millions of tiny pink doughnut-shaped cells in a drop of blood. Incredible. My mind told me it was a pack of lies.'

I smiled, 'But you believe it now, Daudi.'

He nodded, 'I believe it and I know it's true. You showed me how to focus this microscope and then my eye told me another story. You showed me the facts in the pathology book and I discovered that it was not only a thing of interest but a way of finding out how to treat and cure many tropical diseases.'

'Microscopes are handy things, Daudi. They give your eye the opportunity to see tiny things—some beautiful, some dangerous.'

'Look at this slide, Bwana doctor. The sick man I took the blood from has both the small purple rings of malaria and the tiny corkscrew-like *dudus* of tick fever.'

While I examined the blood slide, Daudi picked up an ancient telescope. He focused it. 'Truly telescopes give you the eye of an eagle and distant things become close and clear.'

Suddenly he chuckled, 'One of those who does not understand these things is the man in the yellow shirt, climbing the largest mango tree in the hospital gardens.'

I peered at the dark green patch outlined against the warm brown of the dry river flats. 'My eyes tell me nothing, Daudi.' I picked up the telescope. It was exactly as Daudi had described. 'The man in the yellow shirt has climbed the tree to admire the view!'

Daudi grinned, 'No doubt we shall still be here when he walks past on his way to the village.'

Over a cup of tea we talked about microscopes and telescopes and discussed how they turned the vague distance or the invisibly small into a sharp picture. New beauty is brought to our senses. New safety comes as unseen threats are understood. These instruments make it possible for the mind to grasp many facts that would otherwise be unavailable to it.

I put down the teapot. 'You know, Daudi, faith is like microscopes and telescopes. It makes you understand and know things that your mind could not otherwise grasp. It means putting full confidence in the things we hope for, being certain of things we cannot see' (Hebrews 11:1).

We talked about this for quite a time. Then past the window went a man in a yellow shirt. 'Good afternoon,' he greeted.

'Good afternoon,' we replied.

I asked, 'Did you find the mangoes sweet or sour?'

He raised his eyebrows, 'What mangoes, Doctor?'

'The ones that grew in the hospital garden.'

Yellow shirt smiled as he looked into the distant green haze. 'What magnificent eyes you must have.'

'Come in,' said Daudi, and picked up a stethoscope. This he placed over the middle of the man's stomach and listened intently, 'Truly, I know a mango when I hear one.'

We all laughed, but Daudi was suddenly serious. 'Look through this machine.' He handed over the telescope and made sure the man's eye was open and that the focus was sharp.

A gasp came from yellow shirt. 'I can see the mango trees clearly and behold one in a red shirt now climbs into the branches.'

Daudi looked at me, and the corners of his mouth quivered. 'He too likes to admire the country from a height. Now sit there and we will talk about mangoes later.'

The man squatted in a corner and shook his head, murmuring, 'Who would have thought that distance could have been shortened like that?'

In due course the man in the red shirt walked passed the window. 'Good afternoon,' he greeted.

'Did you find the mangoes sweet or sour?' I asked.

He smiled at me, 'What mangoes, Bwana doctor?'

'The mangoes in the hospital garden.'

'Behold,' said the man, 'those that sit at this window surely have the eyes of vultures.'

The man squatting in the corner sighed, 'They saw you and I saw you too. They have a special machine.'

Daudi picked up the telescope, focused it and a broad grin spread over his face. Before long, red shirt was looking through the telescope. His mouth drooped open. '*Yoh!*' he said, 'Behold I see the tree. There is a man in a white shirt climbing up it.'

- Faith gives substance to our hopes and makes us certain of realities we do not see.

- Faith is confidence.

- Faith is evidence.

- Faith is like title deeds.

- Faith brings into your mind things that you can't see, touch or feel under ordinary conditions.

To the Christian it isn't raw faith that is necessary; it is faith in the Lord Jesus Christ—in his person and his promises.

Trust and obedience are very closely linked. Obedience is the test of your trust in him and also of your love for him.

Faith may be exercised by anybody. It isn't some sort of extra arm that some people are lucky to be born with. It is quite incorrect to feel that you are not the type of person who could have faith. The Bible has only one word for faith and it is the same word that is used for *belief* and for *trust*. It simply means putting all your reliance upon, or wholly committing yourself to, someone.

The Bible does not expect you to put your reliance on or commit yourself to something that is unreasonable.

Faith is not something that is held out as an alternative to using your brains or doing a bit of thinking. When the Bible talks about Jesus Christ as being the Son of God and alive from the dead, it surrounds you with all the evidence that you need. It convinces you that here is a good claim that deserves to be taken seriously.

When John ends his gospel, he says, 'I could have written a whole lot more about what I've been saying, but enough has been said to show you that he is the Son of God and if you put your life into his hands, all will be well' (John 20:31 Author's paraphrase).

The Bible is doing this all the time. Therefore a Christian is not someone who takes the leap in the dark and lands on who-knows-what, but rather someone who responds to the weight of evidence and says, 'That's good enough for me.'

He believes with the kind of belief that the evidence requires.

He puts his whole trust in the Lord Jesus Christ because He's the One around whom the evidence revolves.

You put your faith, your trust, in him and you exercise that faith.

This is the bond that must exist when you ask Jesus to take control. If you don't trust him then there is no relationship. You are merely an observer from a distance.

It is by God's unmerited favour, by grace, that you are saved *through faith.* It is nothing you can achieve. It is God's gift to you.

The classic material on faith is in Hebrews chapter 11, which shows how faith in God works out in the lives of a number of different men and women. What faith *is* and *does* and how it affects your life can be gathered from these quotable quotes from the Bible:

- And without faith it is impossible to please him. The man who approaches God must have faith in two things, first that God exists and secondly that it is worth a man's while to try to find God (Hebrews 11:6 Phillips).

- I pray that out of the glorious richness of his resources he will enable you to know the strength of the Spirit's inner reinforcement—that Christ may actually live in your hearts by your faith (Ephesians 3:16-17 Phillips).

- If you openly admit *by your own mouth* that Jesus Christ is Lord, and if you believe in *your own heart* that God raised him from the dead, you will be saved. For it is believing *in the heart* that makes a man righteous before God, and it is stating his belief by *his own mouth* that confirms his salvation (Romans 10:9-10 Phillips).

- Above all be sure you take faith as your shield, for it can quench every burning missile the enemy hurls at you (Ephesians 6:16 Phillips).

- Belief (faith) can only come from hearing the message, and the message is the word of Christ (Romans 10:17 Phillips).

- So you see, it isn't enough just to have faith. You must also do good to prove that you have it. Faith by itself, if it is not accompanied by action, is dead (James 2:17 NIV).

12
WHICH WAY NOW?
Guidance

The captain of the athletic team was bigger than I was.

He was the school quarter-mile champion.

I generally ran a rather ordinary second to him.

We were to run against two particularly strong teams on a sports track very close to Sydney Harbour. The wind blew hard across the water and the first half of the once-around-the-oval race would be tough going.

My broad-shouldered friend took me aside. 'This is the way we'll run it, Paul. Since it's not being run in tracks, I'll hit the front from the start and you keep close in behind—very close. I'll take the force of that wind. When it's blowing on the side I'll move out a bit and you come into the inside. My part will be to keep the opposition out and I'll give you a special word when you need it. Got it?'

I had.

All went according to plan. He went fast to the front. I ran stride for stride, my shoulders a couple of handbreadths from his. His shoulders were satisfyingly broad. The wind blew his hair about but I was in relatively calm air. We ran a third of the distance this way and then the wind began coming sharply on my cheek. He moved out just enough for me to run to the edge of the track. In his position outside me, anyone who wanted to pass had to run round both of us. This would add yards to the distance to be travelled.

We were past halfway. The wind was helping now. My shadow was a little ahead of his. It stayed that way for a score of strides and then two other new shadows loomed up. My captain's voice came loudly, 'Go now. Keep your stride.'

I ran as fast and as well as I knew how. The finishing line was close. The opposition was breathing almost down my neck. Then came the feather-like touch of the thin piece of wool at the finishing post.

I had won because he went to the front, ran at my side or ran behind me as the need was. He made the pace. He gave the instructions. He was with me all the time.

My responsibility was to do what he planned and to act when he gave the word, using all the skill, all the stamina and all the strength I had.

This produced a win. And so it is with God and us.

The technical word for going God's way is guidance.

Jesus is the author and finisher of our faith. He said to Peter, 'Come, follow me' (Mark 1:17). This applies to you and me just as aptly.

Knowing God's way is important but, first and foremost, know God and know his book.

'Run the race you have to run with patience, your eyes fixed on Jesus, the source and the goal of your faith. Never lose your purpose or your courage' (Hebrews 12:1-3 Author's paraphrase).

When you're on the highway, realise that God has engineered it. You may feel you'd prefer a straight, smooth, shorter route. Remember his path has been surveyed and every step of it travelled by God himself. The grade, the surface, the direction is right for your travel. The purpose is to reach the target that he has selected for you.

He will guide you in the whole length of your life— in the close-up of today and tomorrow and in the long shot of your future.

Keep firmly in front of you the great basic principle, 'Seek first the Kingdom of God and his right way of doing things' (Matthew 6:33 Author's paraphrase).

God's promise is, 'I will instruct you and teach you in the way you should go; I will counsel you and watch over you' (Psalm 32:8).

On your side, you ask for guidance, you seek for it and you knock on doors. God is more willing to show you his plan for you than you are to find it.

His what-to-do-instructions are in Proverbs chapter 3, verses 5 and 6.

Trust in the Lord with all your heart
And lean not on your own understanding;
In all your ways acknowledge him,
AND HE WILL DIRECT YOUR PATH.

Heart, head, hands, and all the rest—feet, ears, eyes, stomach and pocket. Put him first and he will direct your path,

The two great habits that make this possible are:

(a) The habit of regular prayer

(b) The habit of systematic Bible-reading.

He directs your path.

Guidance isn't asking God to endorse the plans that you hold out to him. It is the reverse. You must have your hand out ready to take the blueprint he has drawn up for you. He then expects you to follow this out implicitly.

You cannot expect guidance if you are going against God's way. When you pray, 'Thy kingdom come' realise it involves, 'My kingdom go.'

Guidance covers your everyday routine and the way you deal with emergencies.

It applies also to the wider canvas of your ambition, your job, your marriage, your advancement, your retirement. There is not one area of your life in which God is not prepared to guide you. He promises to guide and instruct us in the many strands that pattern our lives. This includes our ordinary everyday living—routine perhaps, probably far from exciting or frankly dull.

When anything unforeseen happens—a missed train, a flat tyre, a delay like sitting for hours in a waiting room—don't be irritated or upset. Keep your eyes and ears open to whatever opportunity there is and be ready to take it or use the time for a solid session of praying.

This is where the two great habits come into it. We've already looked at 'praying on the hoof.'

Circumstances can be very useful in bringing you guidance.

Your letterbox may well house the information you require. Advertisements in the newspapers or journals may do the same thing.

If you're looking for a job, read what's available and do your part thoroughly in making application.

Sudden sickness or your health pattern may close or open doors. Good medical advice can clarify your action.

Many a person's path has been made clear by listening to a missionary talk, reading a book on practical living or a biography, or by talking to someone who has special experience.

It's valuable to record the facts. Write them down and date them. If you don't run a diary, at least have a *highlights* and *guidelights* record. It can be a great help to your faith at a later stage and it can keep your thinking clear.

Ask for guidance in your routine living. My personal prayer goes something like this; 'Lord, here is today. I'm yours. Please show me what You have for me to do, to say, to write. Help me with the people I meet, the people I treat, the people to whom I talk on the phone, the people I like and the people I don't. Help me to do what You want. Please help me to meet any emergency and to take any opportunity. Please control me through your Holy Spirit.'

If you are in doubt about a thing, don't do it, buy it or say it, till your doubts have been resolved. And that doesn't mean till you've talked yourself into it!

As the Bible puts it, 'Let the peace of God be the umpire in your heart' (Colossians 3:15 Author's paraphrase).

13
LIFE JOB
Career/Ambition

The economics student sat back in his chair. It was obvious that he meant what he was saying. 'Well, doctor, I've become a Christian. Let me go over the matter step by step and see if I have done it as I should. I recognise the disease. I've heard the diagnosis. I admit that it's got its claws into me. I see that nothing I can do can produce a cure, but that Jesus can and will.'

He sat forward. 'Now I've changed my mind about the way I was going. I've asked Jesus to take charge. I understand that I'm forgiven and that I have everlasting life.'

I nodded. 'Yes. You've gone the right way about it and you realise that when God makes a promise He doesn't break it.'

After a moment he smiled. 'And where do I go from here and what do I do—particularly as far as my life-job is concerned?'

Out of our conversation came what follows.

God has a chosen, priority path for everybody in his family to travel. The important thing is to find it and follow it. Into this comes the word *ambition*—the ardent desire to be and to do.

Power, money and prestige—the glittering three. These are everybody's targets, by and large.

Some, however, feel life is futile and purposeless. They ask, 'What is the value in planning for the future?' Look at Luke 19, verse 13 which can well be translated, 'Carry on business actively till I come.'

Some drop out, by way of protest, against the way they feel human society is going. They think dropping out is the only reasonable thing to do. Monasticism is not new, neither is it the normal way of life for the Christian.

Self-service is not the object of a Christian's life. *All* who put their lives into the hands of Jesus the Servant are expected by him to spend their lives in service of some sort.

The practical Christian approach is to use your abilities with the aim of doing your best in the vocation and circumstances God has planned for you.

In finding this preferred plan, a number of factors need to be considered.

You are facing a distance race, not a sprint.

Your life will develop in stages. Your skills, interests and inherent abilities give you at least a pointer to the first stage.

Put all you've got into the effort. Your motive is not mere success but putting God's kingdom and purpose first.

To get on the track of your life-job advice can be very helpful, especially from people who've travelled the road and know the country. Probably your parents will have given much thought to the matter. I suggest you listen to all that is said and think it over carefully. But don't act until you're sure in your own mind that it's the right path in God's sight.

God has promised to direct your path but you must realise that the road is rarely free from ups and downs.

And then there are the dead ends. You may find a particular course of training seems to end in a cul-de-sac, especially at times like graduation. When you come into a place like this, your responsibility is to trust and wait. If you're faced with closed doors, try each handle and give a moderate push. Some doors will open readily. Others won't budge.

But never attack them with an axe or a crowbar. Look over Proverbs 3, verses 5 and 6 again. 'Trust completely in the Lord. Don't lean on your own thinking. In each and every reaction consult and obey him and *he will direct your path*' (Author's paraphrase). You may safely put the emphasis on each of the five last words.

But what if you miss a turning, botch an order or walk past an open door? Is the whole of God's plan for your life ruined?

God has an alternative plan. The clue is in Jeremiah 18. The divine potter shapes a spoiled pot into a new and useful vessel.

The past cannot be changed but it can be confessed, repented of and forgiven.

The question that matters is, 'What should I be doing from this point on?' (Please don't make a habit of botching God's plan and calling for a remould.)

There is no value in debate when God puts a clear sign-post in front of you. Life is too short to experiment in breaking God's law to see what will happen. The sensible thing is to see what happened to men and women whose lives are opened up to you in the Bible.

Look especially at Joseph, Moses, Nehemiah and Daniel. Here are men who took the positive position and became leaders—both national and spiritual. A properly motivated Christian should do better than an equally able person who is a non-Christian. He thinks much less of himself and is, or should be, more dedicated. The result is that he may well gravitate into leadership.

If the affairs of a nation are to be well and honestly run, Christians must not draw back from the responsibilities of leadership if their routine brings them into it.

Your vocation may not take you into a new, dramatic area. But if you're in God's plan you will find scope in which to serve him.

In East Africa our ancient car had broken down in the thornbush jungle. We were five hours from home, and walking. The sun was scorching. We had little to eat and still less to drink.

I sat down in a small patch of shade in a dry riverbed and groaned, 'Nothing but dry sand and cactus.'

'What's up?' asked my friend, Samson.

'Well, to start with, we're short of water.'

He smiled and dug with his hands in the dry sand. A few minutes later he was scooping out water. Then he said, 'Lend me your knife.' He went to a cactus, made a V-shaped cut and soon water was dripping into a cup. He grinned. 'It's there if you look for it, and know your way around.'

If you're allergic to work you won't fit into God's plan.

Read Matthew 25, verses 15 to 30. Jesus spoke the words and they are extremely relevant to you and your life. For talent read approximately $1,000 (£623).

Wherever your job takes you, you are there to be a witness to your Lord—to be his personal representative in that place. As such, make sure you're prepared and skilled in the way to pass on the Good News. It's of primary importance that you're good at your job and that your conduct stands up to the closest examination.

If you come by any or all of the triad of power, money or prestige, regard them and use them simply as a springboard for your witness to your Lord, Jesus Christ.

The worst paid, most opportunity-filled spot in life can be as a minister of a church, or a missionary. Don't side step this life-job without prayer and considerable thought.

14
LIFE PARTNER
Christian Marriage

One of the most important requests to God that you can make is, 'Lord, please lead me to the life-partner of Your choice.'

It is not uncommon that God's answer to this prayer is, 'I have no life-partner for you. To do the special work I've planned for you I need you single.'

This may be for a time or for life. If this is God's plan he brings special opportunities and, if you willingly accept this, he will come more deeply into your life.

Few events have such far-reaching effects on your own life and on others as your marriage.

God makes it clear that his plan is for a *permanent* state.

The great general principles of the matter are clear and need to be tattooed on the hearts of all, both male and female.

In broad focus:

Marry only someone who is a member of God's family. As the Bible puts it—'Do not be yoked together with unbelievers…What fellowship can light have with darkness? What harmony is there between Christ and Belial [the devil]? What does a believer have in common with an unbeliever' (2 Corinthians 6:14-16).

In fine focus:

Success and harmony come from two members of God's family both travelling in the same direction—with similar motives and similar objectives—and both seeking first God's kingdom.

'One standing alone can be conquered. Two can stand back-to-back and conquer. Three is even better, for a triple-braided cord is not easily broken' (Ecclesiastes 4:9-12 Author's Paraphrase). God of course is the third.

Let me underline this for you in African fable fashion.

Monkey and Antelope entered a competition to see who could drag a large stone straightest along the sand of a dry riverbed. They were harnessed with a Y-shaped piece of vine, the stone being attached to the long tail end. Monkey wanted to go on two legs. Antelope on four.

Two different animals with two different ideas.

Result: CHAOS.

Rhino and Hippo were much the same size. They decided to try their luck.

Two different animals, two different approaches.

Result—CHAOS and HEADACHES.

Two giraffes started off with their eyes fixed on a tree in the far distance. They started off from a kneeling position. They walked together in step. Their path was straight.

Make sure that these principles are crystal clear in your mind as well as inscribed in your heart. This will obviously mean that you have close friendship and fellowship with Christians. When people are in love they throw prudence to the winds. They frequently ask for advice and only rarely take it. They rationalise as follows:

'But it's different in our case.'

'We're the exception that proves...'

'I shall help him to understand...'

'She isn't a Christian yet but when we are married...'

There are at least one hundred other well-known 'yes-buts' and none of them works.

This line of thinking leads to trouble, sadness, heartbreak and varying degrees of ineffectiveness.

You can't go against God and get away with it.

I end as I began. Make your regular prayer, 'Lord, please lead me to the life-partner of Your choice.'

15
HIP POCKET NERVE
Money

Money is not the root of all evil—but the LOVE of it is. Money used with the love of God in your heart and a willing and obedient hand in the pocket can produce splendid results.

On the other side of the coin, the misuse of money can, and does, produce severe soul-sickness.

Compared with giving your complete obedience and loyalty to your Lord, giving your money is in a very much lesser class.

Jesus said, 'For where your treasure is, there your heart will be also' (Matthew chapter 6:21). In the light of this it is interesting to feel the cold hush that comes over people when you start talking about giving.

Your attitude to your finances is like the mercury in a thermometer. Take a reading of your soul's temperature. If the reading is LUKEWARM, COLD,

VERY COLD or ZERO, what about a bit of action and change of attitude?

The Bible says, 'It is more blessed to give than to receive' (Acts 20:35).

God has a number of clear-cut, practical things to say about the uses of money and the way you can employ it.

It is not the highly important matter that it seems but it has a part of its own to play. This 'do-what-God-says-about-money' is often called the *stewardship of money*.

Total assets

This refers to your material holding in things and cash: your income, your capital, all you've got. Proverbs 3, verse 9 reads, 'Honour the Lord with your wealth.' This covers the whole situation.

But what does 'honour' mean?

Part of the answer is, 'Bring the whole tithe into the storehouse, that there may be food in my house' (Malachi 3:10).

A tithe is a tenth—10 percent. This I regard as the minimum percentage of income to give.

The principle is planned, systematic, proportionate giving. Paul gives the clue in 1 Corinthians 16, verse 2. Following this through takes the fangs out of money loving.

I suggest that you look at the most convenient time period which covers your own income. My own way of dealing with the situation is once a year to estimate my income, work out its net value and to give at least 10 percent. (This is the *first* 10 percent not the last, which probably will be eroded by expenses.) Then I plan a monthly gift to a number of organisations. This includes my local church, the Christian organisations that have greatly helped and influenced my own life and that of my family, missionaries and missionary societies, and some special work or individuals that have crossed my path.

This is documented, done regularly and revised at least annually.

But giving a proportion of your income is not enough if you leave it just at money. Jesus talks to the scribes and Pharisees and says, 'Alas for you … you utter frauds. For you pay your tithe on mint and aniseed and cumin, and neglect the things which carry far more weight in the Law—justice, mercy and good faith. These are the things you should have observed—without neglecting the others' (Matthew 23:23 Phillips).

Generosity

This is a good thing but at times it can be irresponsible and as a Christian you are a responsible person. Planned generosity is far better. Giving to appeals, emotional or otherwise, Christian or secular, should come from your own pocket and not from the proportions that you have put on one side for God.

Wills

Some wise man remarked that there are no pockets in a shroud. There is much more satisfaction in giving while your soul is in your body. At the same time there is value in not forgetting to make your will. I made mine very close to my twenty-first birthday and have revised it from time to time making sure that such as I have is suitably taken care of and shared out in the way that I should wish. It is a good idea to ask the help of a Christian lawyer. This I regard as good stewardship.

God doesn't penalise those who lock their purses and pockets, as far as he is concerned, while they concentrate on building up their own finances. The fact is that they don't give God the opportunity to bless them.

The eagerness to pile up money may well swing God out of the centre of their living. Jesus pointed out, 'You cannot serve God and the power of money at the same time' (Matthew 6:24 Phillips).

Very often when God speaks of giving he has something more to say which amounts to a bonus or promise. The currency may be different but the blessing is real and great.

God delights to bless you. There is real adventure in giving to him.

In all three verses we have considered as guidelines to giving, there is this special blessing attachment.

Look at them:

Malachi 3, verse 10: 'Test me in this, says the Lord Almighty, and see if I will not throw open the floodgates of heaven and pour out so much blessing that you will not have room enough for it.'

Proverbs 3, verses 9-11: 'Honour the Lord with your wealth, with the firstfruits of all your crops; then your barns will be filled to overflowing, and your vats will brim over with new wine.'

Matthew 6, verse 33: 'Set your heart on his kingdom and his goodness, and all these things will come your way as a matter of course' (Phillips). God knows your needs.

You give to God because you love him, not because you expect something back.

'Let the man who is called to give, give freely' (Romans 12:8 Phillips).

If you have a flair for business, well and good. Go to it. (Christian outreach needs to be financed). There is also scope for explaining to others what God says about money.

It is wise to remember Jesus' quiet warning, 'When you give to the needy, do not let your left hand know what your right hand is doing.' (Matthew 6:3) There is no future in patting your hip pocket so loudly that others will take notice.

As I said earlier, there is danger in loving money.

Conveniently, in parts of East Africa, the coins used to have a hole bored through the centre...

A certain monkey with keen love for money saw his wealth grow as his threaded-coin necklace became longer and longer. To avoid requests for a loan from his many friends and relations, he attempted to cross a shallow river. Unfortunately he was unaware of a wide hole dug in the riverbed. Down he went head-

over-heels. The money anchored him headfirst to the bottom.

His common sense told him, 'Monkey, break the string and live.'

His monkey wisdom which is much the same thing as love of money said still louder, 'What, and lose all your wealth?'

The dialogue became more urgent. 'Break the string and breathe.'

'And lose all you've battled for? All your lovely money?'

His head sank deeper.

The first voice grew softer; the second kept on, 'Money, money, your money.'

Then came silence, deep silence.

Days later, monkey's legs were found sticking up through the mud.

The jungle summary of the situation was, 'What an unsatisfactory end to a life; to be anchored by a lot of money, head-first in the bottom of a mud hole.'

Some more thoughtful monkeys even asked, 'What good did his money do to him down there?'

Money can bring a variety of hazards and troubles.

Covetousness

God gave a whole commandment to this subject. It means a greedy longing to get your hands on what belongs to someone else. It is love of someone else's money.

Coveting is a trap to keep well away from. It is said to be the sin to which no one confesses.

Greed

'A greedy man brings trouble to his family' (Proverbs 15: 27).

Greed makes it possible to have the things money can buy while you lose the things that money can't buy.

Debt

My personal advice is to keep out of certain varieties of debt.

Buying a house with borrowed money is a wise move. Repayment to a bank or building society costs little more than rent.

Going into debt to keep up with the Joneses - a new car, all the electrical servants, the latest in IT

(Information Technology) - this is bad stewardship. Save up and avoid credit card debt. Buy as you're able and you will add greatly to the fun of setting up a new home. Being in debt can make it difficult, if not impossible, to move when God might want you elsewhere.

Before you make a big spend, check on your giving to God. Record this for your own information. You'll be surprised how much less your giving is than you think.

Gambling

There is no direct mention of gambling in the Bible (the same is true of television!) but there is much said about jealousy, envy and covetousness.

'He that makes haste to be rich shall not be innocent,' says Proverbs 28:20 (Author's paraphrase).

Gambling has the aim of quick money without work and reward without effort.

This habit-forming, compulsive approach stimulates 'love of money' and has no place in a Christian's financial dealings.

Gambling is as useful a pastime to a Christian as going for a stroll in a minefield.

Security (of the financial kind)

There is no such animal.

Read what Paul said to Timothy about money:

'There is a real profit, of course, but it comes only to those who live contentedly as God would have them live...

'For men who set their hearts on being wealthy expose themselves to temptation. They fall into one of the world's traps, and lay themselves open to all sorts of silly and wicked desires, which are quite capable of utterly ruining and destroying their souls. For loving money leads to all kinds of evil, and some men in the struggle to be rich have lost their faith and caused themselves untold agonies of mind...

'Set your heart not on riches, but on goodness, Christ-likeness, faith, love, patience and humility. Fight the worthwhile battle of the faith, keep your grip on that life eternal to which you have been called' (1 Timothy 6:6, 9-12 Phillips).

16
WRONG ROAD
Sin

'You say that going God's way is dynamite,' said the radio personality.

He was expert in bringing conflict into an interview and putting the man on the other side of the microphone on the spot.

I nodded, 'Yes, that has been my experience as a doctor in East Africa and wherever else I have lived. There's tremendous satisfaction in God's way of life but you need to have a go at it to understand.'

He leaned forward, 'Tell me about it.'

I told him how a medical missionary's work made a considerable difference to people's bodies and souls.

His eyes hardened. 'I like your stories, Doctor, but why do you and many of those like you always talk so much about sin, sin, sin?'

I came back at him hard. 'I'm a doctor. My job is to fight disease and its results in man's body and mind—the misery, pain, suffering, weakness, confusion, death. What you mustn't forget or overlook is that sin is the disease of man's soul, a deadly thing.'

There was an odd twist at the corner of his mouth, 'Don't you think that all this talk about sin is vastly overdone?'

'Not if you take any notice of what God has to say about it. People shut their eyes and ears to the facts. They especially fail to face up to God's statement that we are all involved and infected. And we are all in the same boat. Apart from God's help sin is incurable. Nothing that we can do ourselves has any effect. Achievement counts for nothing. This is where God's power comes into the picture. Jesus Christ has the complete answer to the disease and all it produces. He himself is the cure—the only cure.'

The radio personality's voice came smoothly in, 'How interesting.'

He touched a button and addressed the microphone, 'Now let's have a little music.'

Sin is an unpopular subject. The more realistically it's spoken about the more unpopular it is, especially if there is any mention of the sting in its tail.

It is acceptable to very many only if it is in technicolour, deodorised and called something quite different.

Sin is the tree. Sins are the fruit.

Look at the tree; take a wide view.

SIN

- is a corruption of the human heart, a profound disorder of human nature that refuses to be tamed or set right.
- is a determination to be independent of God and to plan and travel our own road regardless of him.
- is telling God to go and mind his own business.

We have turned in on ourselves and chosen not to be the kind of people God wants us to be.

We are completely unable to change that condition from within ourselves.

We are trapped by our problem.

Look at the tree in close-up.

SIN

- is coming short of God's standard.

- is missing the target God has set up.

- is doing what you know to be wrong.

- is not doing what you know to be right.

- may smell like fun, but follow it through and it stinks of corruption.

You can't free yourself of either fruit or tree by hacking at the trunk or lopping off the limbs. The more enthusiastically you prune, the stronger the tree grows and the more fruit it produces.

   The one and only answer to the situation is that the whole sinister tree must be dealt with—root, trunk and branch. This you cannot do by yourself. The only One who can is the Lord Jesus Christ and he is completely capable and willing.

There is the story of the African children who found a baby leopard and fed it consistently on porridge, nothing but porridge. Never even a small bit of meat.

They found, very uncomfortably, that little leopards

become big leopards and big leopards kill.

Then there is the matter of the small monkeys who said they didn't believe in crocodiles.

'They're like dragons,' they scoffed. 'Thought up to scare us and interfere with our freedom.'

They found out fast and sadly that if we say there are no crocodiles we deceive ourselves.

Look at what John has to say. 'If we claim to be

without sin, we deceive ourselves and the truth is not in us' (1 John 1:8). A few verses later on comes the great answer. 'He (Jesus) is the atoning sacrifice for our sins, and not only for ours but also for the sins of the whole world' (1 John 2:2).

Those who play down sin's deadliness often come out with the statement, 'God is too kind and loving to punish people.'

Sin is no fun-word to God.

To God sin is so serious that he gave his Son to die a criminal's death to be the one and only way of forgiveness.

The cost to God was infinite. The price to us is nothing. Closing our minds to this forgiveness is the supreme sin.

God does not punish us for our sins. He loves us so greatly that he makes this great freedom ours for the asking. If we reject his unique cure, the responsibility lies not with the One who supplies the way out, but with the one who neglects to take it.

17
KNOW YOUR ENEMY
Temptation/Devil

We sometimes joke about the devil.

But the devil was no joke to Peter, who called him, 'your enemy ... like a roaring lion looking for someone to devour' (1 Peter 5:8).

The devil was no joke to Paul, who wrote, 'Put on the full armour of God so that you can take your stand against the devil's schemes' (Ephesians 6:11).

The Lord Jesus Christ spoke of the devil as a personal agent of evil.

Get away from the cartoon figure with horns, hooves and pronged tail and see the enemy as he is—active, destructive, malicious, implacable and utterly hostile.

He is particularly hostile to you. Your fight is not against a physical enemy but against organisations and powers that are spiritual; against unseen powers that are spiritual. Spiritual agents from the very headquarters of evil.

The devil is variously called a murderer from the beginning, the inspirer of wars and crime, the father of lies, the manipulator of dissension and division. The devil is the accuser. He accuses men before God and he accuses God to men. He whispers that God does not care, that he doesn't do what he promises.

When you have doubts that you have really been forgiven or that your prayers are being heard—that's the devil accusing. Our adversary is more than wily. He has more forms of outreach than an octopus. He knows all the cunning ways to tempt the senses.

The background music and the subtle fragrance are all planned to make you take small notice of what really goes on. In mellow tones he asks, 'How could there be problems in a wide, smooth, well-grassed, colourfully-flowered slope?'

Make no mistake. There is an unexpected chasm ahead with a long, long, deadly drop.

The enemy is delighted if he can camouflage himself and keep his activities out of sight. He has scored well if he can convince you that he doesn't exist and make you think this suggestion is your own idea and not really off-key. This gives him a considerable advantage.

So much the better for him and so much the worse for you.

Why shouldn't you do your own thing anyhow?

The enemy is a master of his own particular variety of sales talk. He's a mimic and he can throw his voice in all directions. He is the prince of hidden persuaders.

'Delicious,' he whispers, and it explodes in your face.

'You've never tasted anything like it,' comes his wheedling undertone.

Buy it and you're in for gastric discomfort, which makes seasickness, and the whole family of the dysenteries seem like a picnic, quite apart from the deep, gnawing ache, which goes on and on.

It always seems to me a pity that we can't hear the hellish laughter of the enemy and his subtle salesmen, when we're unwise enough to let those whispers get a grip on our thinking.

One of the Jungle Doctor fable-yarns tells the story of a small monkey who lived in his buyu tree. He had been advised by his monkey uncle and his wise friend giraffe not to let vultures settle on his family tree.

'You can't stop them circling above it,' they told him, 'But the big thing is to throw stones at them and not bones. NEVER encourage vultures.'

But small monkey liked the danger game. He was convinced that he could get away with it and he threw bones and found disaster.

You can't stop temptation coming to your ears but it's vital that you stop it from seeping into your thoughts and into your living.

Reject it at the source and you prevent temptation from becoming sin. There is positive value in throwing stones at the vultures.

It's important to realise that God does not tempt you to sin, because he has nothing to do with evil. Man's temptation is due to the pull of his inward desires and these can be tremendously attractive. When his desire gets a grip, sin results. And sin in the long run means death.

And what does the enemy do when you buy what he has so skillfully suggested? He records in your dossier the fact that you'll fall for this and that, and he notes the way in which he will work the same trick next time. It may be straight, raw temptation. It may be the same temptation in a different shape or size, scent or flavour.

He will kick you when you're down and produce a collection of such logical-sounding lies that you'll believe the lot. He will use his clinical voice and tell you, 'There. You've done it. You're done for.'

It's a lie. Jesus will forgive you again and again to the very end of the road if you come asking for that

102

forgiveness. Of course you don't deserve it. That's what grace is—a gift of great value that you don't deserve.

How can you get the better of temptation?

It takes time for an egg to hatch, so don't sit on temptation. Kick it out of your nest as fast as you can.

God's book is no mere formality. What it says, works.

In our kitchen is a tube of yellow ointment. I burnt my finger on the side of a frying pan that didn't look hot but was viciously so. I checked the label on the ointment tube. It read: *For Burns*. I applied it to my finger. The pain stopped. It was true to label.

And God's book is infinitely more so. He says in James 4 verse 6 that he resists the proud person, but gives grace to the humble man. The thing is to be humble before God but resist the devil and he will run away from you. Come close to God and he will come close to you (James 4:7-8).

A modern line in diabolic persuasion is—*conform*. Be a member of the 'now' generation. Forget the past; don't think about the future. Live for now. But God's book says, 'Don't let the world around you squeeze you into its mould, but let God remould your minds from within' (Romans 12:2 Phillips).

Temptation is to do as others do, in the way that all the rest do it, in the matter of standards and behaviour.

Members of God's family are often tempted to think principally of Christian *feeling*—to focus their mind on what God can do for them.

Personal benefits are there but they're interest, not capital. We serve God because he is God. What *feels* great is one thing; what is God's mind and will for us may be quite another.

Prove in practice that the plan of God for you is good. God wants to be in the centre of your life, not out towards the edge of it.

There is a delightful notice outside a wild animal park that abounds with lions; it says '*Trespassers will be eaten*,' and then advises that there is no risk if you stay at all times inside your car.

Stay close to God. Keep your communications open. Keep reading his book. Make friends with Christians and take advantage of fellowship with them. Keep out of the reach of temptation and the things which make it easier for temptation to reach your ears and thinking.

Small monkey made his great mistake by storing up bones to throw to his vultures.

I am just returning two books to the library, largely unread. They contain stuff which would only make it easier for temptation to hatch.

The same is true of some television shows and films, magazines of a certain type, some newspapers and posters, internet dangers and pornographic displays in shop windows. I don't have to list them for you.

There is positive danger in storing up bones. If you do this, don't blame the enemy. Remember that it's you who make the decisions. The devil and his human dupes advertise and promote the goods, but *you* buy them.

There's always great value in seeing what the Lord Jesus Christ did when he was tempted (Matthew chapter 4). Note how he used the Bible as a weapon. Follow his lead. Read the technique in Ephesians 6, verses 10 to 18:

'Be strong—not in yourselves but in the Lord, in the power of his boundless resource...' (Phillips).

Peter, whose mistakes and temptation have been listed in the Bible to help you to avoid doing the same thing wrote, 'So, humble yourselves under God's strong hand, and in his own good time he will lift you up. You can throw the whole weight of your anxieties upon him, for you are his personal concern.

'Be self-controlled and vigilant always, for your enemy the devil is always about, prowling like a lion roaring for its prey. Resist him, standing firm in your faith, and remember that the strain is the same for all your fellow Christians in other parts of the world' (1 Peter 5:6-9 Phillips).

18
DANGER AHEAD
Warnings

The headlights were gone. The bodywork was pushed crazily to one side. The windscreen was shattered.

From the wreck struggled a man covered with blood. Before he slipped into unconsciousness he muttered out his story to the ambulance driver, 'Collected a 'roo—big as a bull, it was.'

I worked on him for three hours in the small bush hospital in western Queensland.

Next morning he was swathed in bandages, his arm in a sling and his leg in plaster. His only visible eye was bruised, puffy and red.

'How many stitches, Doc?' he muttered through swollen lips.

'Forty-nine, and I found three of your front teeth had been knocked out. Your bruising is magnificent. What exactly happened?'

'I was driving along that long, straight stretch five miles out of town, when there he was in my headlights. He jumped right at me, WHAM! I stopped two hundred pounds of red kangaroo.'

'Were you going fast?'

There was a touch of pride in his husky voice. 'Foot on the floor, Doc.'

'But didn't you see the *Beware of 'roos* notice?'

'I've seen it a hundred times. Didn't think it could happen to me.'

The trim, clear-cut warning notice didn't go into details of surgery, X-rays, damage, pain and disability. But it was all there for those who cared to realise that it could happen to them.

That's the first half—half the don't-shut-your-mind-to-facts story.

The second half happened to me when I was having my hair cut.

There is nothing much to look at during this operation. In the mirror, I watched the barber strike a match to light the limp, homemade cigarette, which dangled on his lower lip. When this had reached the stage where it would no longer stay in place, he put down his scissors and comb and proceeded to roll another weary cigarette. My medical interest was centred on the spot where that moist collection of paper and tobacco had been resting. As the barber continued clipping away I said, 'Excuse me, but that thing on your lip—have you ever had a doctor look at it?'

He stopped and faced me, 'Why should I?'

'Well, I've seen things like that before. Watch it. Take my tip and have it fixed up.'

As I paid him he said, 'You're a doctor, are you?' I nodded.

In due course I returned. He greeted me with a smile. 'Well,' I said, 'did you see that doctor?'

He shook his head, 'I had a better idea. Look at this.' He held out a six-inch, amber holder. In it was the inevitable home-rolled cigarette. As he worked I noticed the holder rested over the same spot on his lip. One glance made it clear that the condition had worsened since I had last seen it.

'I'm afraid your holder won't do much to help your lip. You'd be wise to see the skin specialist I told you about. If you like I'll write you a letter of introduction.'

He shrugged, 'Oh, it'll be all right.'

'Listen! It won't be all right. From my experience I know that this is a highly dangerous condition. Don't fool with it. Get the thing fixed up properly.' I was a little brusque in my manner.

He stopped to light another cigarette. There was an edge on his voice. 'Listen mate, it's mine. I'll look after it.'

I went home that afternoon and took from my shelf a book which described and pictured the variety of early cancer from which he was suffering. The illustration could have been an actual photograph of that barber's lip.

Putting the book under my arm, I walked up to his shop. I waited till he had no customers and showed him the whole thing. I told him, 'This is the standard text book on this sort of cancerous growth.'

He studied the picture and compared it with his own lip, looking at it carefully in the mirror. After a time he said, 'It does look like what I've got, doesn't it?'

I showed him the grim word, *epithelioma*, and pointed to the paragraph where it explained the end result of his trouble. It told in plain medical terms that if untreated death would result.

We talked this over. He listened carefully and said, 'Well, thanks, I'll think about it.'

On my way home I thought, 'I've done what I can. I've warned him about it. I've told him what I know from my own experience and I've shown it to him in the standard textbook. Now it is up to him to take action.'

When my next haircut was due he greeted me with a knowing look. 'I've fixed it all right. Doc. I had a bottle of corn cure in the cupboard. I put it on for three days and the top came off it and now you wouldn't notice it was there. It looks like a brand new lip.'

It didn't to me. The vicious swelling was horribly obvious.

I felt under his chin and down his neck. The glands were slightly swollen and hard.

I shook my head; 'Corn cure is only setting your mind at rest. You're doing no good to this thing, and you're running the greatest risk. It may look all right to you but the root of the trouble is there. Do the sensible thing. Get that lip fixed up.'

I left the shop and a week later moved to another district.

Six months went by. I had reason to visit the town again. I thought I'd drop in and see my barber friend.

A new barber came to meet my needs. 'Good morning,' I said. 'Where is the man who used to run this shop?'

He shook his head, 'That's rather an unhappy story, sir. I regret to tell you that it was only a couple of weeks ago that he died. He had cancer of the lip.'

I told this incident to a friend, a medical man, who had never taken any interest when I had talked to him about God.

Said my friend, 'It was his own fault. He took no notice of your experience and more important still he shrugged off what he had seen and read in the book.'

'Watch it,' I said. 'You're not so very different from that barber. You, he and every one of us has a deadly disease which affects the soul. The complete cure is available to everybody.'

He shrugged and firmly changed the subject.

To round off the Sermon on the Mount, Jesus told a clear-cut story of two men.

He starts, 'Everyone who hears these words of mine and puts them into practice is like a sensible man who built his house on the rock. The storm came: rain, wind, floods. That house did not fall. Its foundation was rock.

'Everyone who hears these words of mine and does not follow them is like a foolish man who built his house on sand. The storm came: rain, wind, floods battered that house. It fell with a great crash' (Matthew 7, verses 24:27 Author's paraphrase).

'Don't be under any illusion: you cannot make a fool of God! A man's harvest in life will depend entirely on what he sows. If he sows for his own lower nature his harvest will be the decay and death of his own nature. But if he sows for the Spirit he will reap the harvest of everlasting life by the Spirit' (Galatians 6:7-8 Phillips).

We ought to pay the greatest attention to the truth that we have heard and not allow ourselves to drift away from it (Hebrews 2:1 Phillips).

19
HELL-SMELLS
The Occult

Talking about the devil . . .

Earlier on you met my Science Master who was an odd type, always talking about things that were on the fringe of science and leaving us to work out the rudiments of chemistry ourselves. Occasionally he would burst into activity and words. One such day he saw a curly-headed character (later to become a criminal lawyer) at the chemical cupboard, furtively handling a bottle of red substance. He was about to add it to a jar already containing yellow, white and black powders. A glass rod was handily placed for the mixing process. Science Master's rather dreamy voice was for once rather sharp, 'My lad, NEVER—and that means NOT EVER—NEVER, use that material for what I presume you intend to do.'

Gingerly he lowered the lot into a bucket of water.

'Silly ass,' I thought. 'Making gunpowder, eh? Fancy shoving that collection into a jam jar and stirring it.

He'd be lucky not to blow himself through the skylight and take a few others with him.'

The more I thought about it, the more I thought how different it would be in my hands. I realised the risks and could avoid them easily by exercising suitable care. Gunpowder was fascinating stuff if you watched your step. I felt sure old Bill's *never* routine didn't apply in my case.

I bought the ingredients and carried them home, separately of course, in a very commonsense way.

It was pleasing to know that my mother was out.

Measuring and mixing was performed with considerable care.

Even greater caution was called for in transferring the final result to a large and very clean test tube and sealing it. Then came the great moment. I tossed my experiment into the brick incinerator. This solid but unlovely edifice split open with a roar. Half a brick sailed through a fibrous-cement outhouse. A window was shattered. A sheet of flame belched out at me. I lost a lot of hair and one eyebrow, and acquired a deep gash in my scalp. Dry grass and a pile of wood caught fire. It took hours with the hose and woodworking tools to make even partial repairs.

As the doctor stitched me up, he told me in no uncertain terms about others who had played with gunpowder and its relations. Starkly he described the results as he had seen them.

You can't play with the devil and not touch disaster.

For hundreds of years in all parts of the world people have had anti-devil potions, charms and all the rest of it to give them some sense of freedom from fear.

In Africa I saw a whole network of rituals designed to cope with the pressure that the *mapepo*, the spirits (mainly hostile), bring to bear on their everyday living. Charms were worn round the neck, the waist, hung from the ears, plaited into the hair, worn round the ankles or swallowed.

In our own so-called sophisticated culture the same thing is true in a not very different way. People have private rituals, whether it is touching wood, throwing salt over the shoulder, taking rabbits' feet to an examination or wearing good luck charms with their own particular sign of the zodiac.

Currently people are feeling that the devil and the demonic is a much bigger factor than they had previously thought and they are moving from superstition and charms into a much wider activity. We are in the area of ouija boards, séances, the occult and black masses.

Folk at universities are experimenting in Satanism. There are those who have committed themselves to the devil. Films, the press, paperbacks, the theatre are stimulating interest in the occult.

Many who have been bored with what the Bible calls 'the flesh'—illicit sex, perversion, drugs, alcohol (one in ten social drinkers becomes an alcoholic)—turn to the occult.

The road sign is not only *Stop* but *Go back, you are on the wrong road*.

Don't touch any phase of the occult.

Watch out for two dangerous traps.

The first is not to believe that Satan and his forces exist.

The second is becoming fascinated with the occult.

TRAP ONE

'If we can convince them that we don't exist we are halfway to victory.' This is a paraphrase of the words C.S. Lewis puts into the mouth of Screwtape, the master tempter.

There is no doubt from the Bible that the Lord Jesus believed in devils. Satan is called the enemy, the adversary. He opposes all that is for the glory of God or for the blessing of men.

If God is for a thing, the devil is against it. He throws all he has into the conflict. He stirs opposition in every way to any forward movement for the work of God and of people who are going God's way.

He battles to keep people from coming to God. He is described in a number of pictorial ways.

He opposes, he divides, he corrupts. He may appear as an angel of light, but he is counterfeit. He's ingenious, he's underhanded, a slanderer.

He has every shot in the locker.

For us the matter for encouragement is that we have the whole armour which enables us to cope with all his approaches. Ephesians 6, verse 11 gives you the information you require. Look it up. File it in your memory.

Further encouragement is, 'your enemy the devil prowls…Resist him …after you have suffered a little while, God … will himself restore you and make you strong, firm and steadfast. To him be the power for ever and ever' (1 Peter 5:8-11).

Don't fiddle with any of the devil's tools or play with any of the explosive toys he offers so enticingly. See what God has to say about them. There is nothing permissive about it.

These are handily listed for you in the book of Deuteronomy chapter 18, verse 10 and the verses that follow.

You are forcibly advised against these things. It is useful to have a mental grip of what they are.

'None of you must practice divination.' *Divination* is to find out events in the future by trance or second sight or using some device. In ancient times, augury referred to examination of the liver or intestines of a sacrifice. In modern times tea leaves are a less smelly substitute.

In Africa, just as back in Old Testament times, sticks, arrows and sandals were thrown into the air and, according to the way they pointed, people worked out the likelihood of success in hunting, in battle or in love. God is against it. He says the man who does these things is detestable. You find the mention of sorcery, the use of charms, the consultation of ghosts or spirits. To all of these things God says 'DON'T' with great clarity.

Necromancy means called up the dead, being controlled by a familiar spirit, being a medium or running a séance. Again this is a thing which God says he hates. If he hates it and you say you love him, you should have nothing to do with the occult.

Few newspapers are printed without reference to 'your stars.' Astrology has a tremendous grip. Astrologers draw conclusions from the position of the sun, the moon and the planets. The Bible does not speak kindly of this line of activity. The broad outline as you will read it in the Old Testament is: Don't follow people who make horoscopes and who try to read their fate and future in the stars. Their ways are futile and foolish.*

Wizards, witches, séances—all the rest of it—they have no place in your life and they can tear strips off your Christian witness, making it futile and ineffective.

TRAP TWO

Trap two has a very wide coverage and can tickle the imagination. It is most carefully and skillfully baited with all the right tastes and smells. Don't become intrigued by the occult. If you do you can easily find yourself either knocked about or the edge taken from

---

* See Isaiah 47:10-15

your interest in God's way. It is not difficult to be mentally blackmailed by this fifth column, the avowed enemies of God and of his kingdom.

The enemy may take more captives with quiet subversion than he will by frontal attacks. Much of the talk about witchcraft and its side issues has been seen to distract people from the basic purpose of Christian living. There is no value in following this particularly ripe red herring.

Our task is not to explain the devil and demons and to expose their various tricks but rather to proclaim the Lord Jesus Christ's victory over them.

We need to know our enemy but most of all to concentrate on our Lord.

20
THE MANUFACTURER'S INSTRUCTIONS
Sex

Have you ever spilt a cup of tea on the tablecloth? It looks like a bucketful, makes an awful mess and the flavour, the warmth and the refreshment are gone. This is what happens when a good thing is in the wrong place.

God made sex to give added happiness and effectiveness in the closest human partnership of all. Sex in marriage can be very good. God planned it and designed it. We can and should thank him for every bit of sexuality we possess. In the Bible God gives 'the manufacturer's advice' on the whole situation.

'If,' said the brochure on the pop-up toaster, 'you find this very useful and sophisticated device does not work, may we suggest that you read the manufacturer's instructions? Do not bring any metallic object into contact with the element.'

These instructions have real positive value. They

say *don't*, so as to produce better results and greater satisfaction—as well as to preserve your personal safety.

The Bible has much to say about sex. Clear-cut instruction—all of it designed to bring out the best from this complex and unique gift.

'Let your lives be living proofs of the things which please God. Steer clear of the activities of darkness; let your lives show by contrast how dreary and futile these things are' (Ephesians 5: 10-11 Phillips).

In a score of places there are signposts to keep you on the right road: No fornication; No adultery; No dirty-mindedness; No foul talk; No perversion; No homosexual activity.

Many think actions are all that matters.

Jesus makes it clear that to think evil is on a par with doing evil. People may be respectable in what they do and be highly regarded because of this. But inside (in what the Bible calls the heart) there may be vicious thoughts, impure thoughts, bitter thoughts.

Jesus indicates that purity is the essential passport to the kingdom of God. The pure in heart shall see God.

He said, 'Anyone who looks at a woman lustfully has already committed adultery with her in his heart' (Matthew 5:28). Jesus has nothing against the sheer pleasure that there is in looking at a beautiful person, but he strongly condemns the looking that is designed to awaken desire and passion.

You need to know about sex. Not the jig-saw picture that you piece together from the things written on the back of lavatory doors, heard in coarse jokes, or read furtively in magazines and books. You need the facts. Everything is to be said for knowing the whole picture.

The sexual revolution of the 1960s promised fun and freedom. It's the same today. The slogan is, 'If it feels good, do it.' But as in most revolutions the casualties outnumber the gains. Whether you're married or single, this big lie can slash deep into your life.

The Bible gives the guidelines to how each person's sexual life is to be lived. For single people there is no doubt that God's way is: 'No sexual intercourse till marriage.' For married folk it is just as clear-cut: 'No sexual intercourse except in your marriage.'

Currently chastity and fidelity have lost popularity. There are many films and novels which display the opposite view. In them, living outside God's commands is commended to us because the story ends happily. Stress is laid on any heart-warming event with the soft pedal on sorrow or injury.

There is little mention of people whose lives have been crippled or shipwrecked on the way. Little is said about those who are profoundly influenced by the happenings. This includes the damage done to children who are caught in the crossfire.

There is a web of intersecting detail and heartache in true life, which is conveniently left out of the script. However, you meet them only too starkly and only too often in medical practice.

You cannot break God's laws about sex without doing havoc to yourself and to others. God judges our lives on their total effect all the time.

King David—an experienced and mature man, a soldier, a poet, a musician, a hero and a father of many children—fell for the trap.

Looking through his window he saw a beautiful woman bathing. He fed his fantasies and kept looking. He was hooked by the temptation.

To achieve his ends he planned a murder and carried it through with bitter, long-term results. Scores of people were involved in the backlash of this disobedience to God's instruction. Over went commandment seven ('You shall not commit adultery') to be followed quickly by commandment six ('You shall not murder'), and commandments eight and ten ('You shall not steal' and 'You shall not covet') were shattered in the breaking of the other two.

What happened to King David happens inevitably to anyone else who follows the same path. Solomon was the son of this union. He wrote: 'Can a man scoop fire into his lap without his clothes being burned? Can a man walk on hot coals without his feet being scorched? So is he who sleeps with another man's wife; no one who touches her will go unpunished' (Proverbs 6:27-29).

Marriage does not automatically do away with sexual temptation. In times of difficulty particularly, the devil is adept at turning the mind in other directions, suggesting that someone else is more attractive. Don't fall into his trap. Keep God's signposts in clear view.

Be cautious about feeding your fantasies.

Do you find it hard to keep your thinking clear?

Do you find it uncomfortably easy to remember the rude joke or the vulgar incident in a book or film or T.V. show?

Why shovel dirt into your memory when you want it to be clean? It is infinitely hard to scrub scenes and thoughts out of your mind. It's so very easy to put them in.

'How can a young man keep his way pure? By living according to your word' (Psalm 119:9).

If you're courting or going out with someone, the following problem will arise:

How far do we go with physical contact? The answer needs to be worked out and decided when you're not emotionally involved in the situation.

If you first think about this while you're at the end of a date, parked in the dark, it could be too late. You don't wait to consult a sea chart until after you hear the surf beating on the rocks! Avoiding trouble is always worthwhile. Keep in mind the monkeys who knew that vultures should be kept flying and not allowed to land on their tree.

The practical solution was to throw stones to keep the vicious birds in the air and in no way to encourage them.

Making a habit of reading, talking and looking at sexually stimulating material fattens your fascinations and makes your defences flabby.

Put muscle round your soul by nourishing it from God's book. In this battle the better-fed part of you wins the battle of your mind.

God is not down on pleasant physical sensation. But he is concerned with what's happening in our hearts and heads. If you find yourself wanting to give in to sexual temptation, to give yourself sexual pleasure in any way when you are not married then beware. God wants us to be more stable than that.

Don't say, 'I won't do it again.' Keep your eyes on Jesus and let him change your life pattern. Talk to Jesus about your sex problems as in all other areas of your life. He won't be shocked. You haven't done anything he doesn't know all about.

The Bible has the most forcible things to say about *perversion*. Homosexuality and other perverse sexual practices are absolutely forbidden. See Leviticus 18, verse 22 and 23. The strongest terms are used.

I have the advantage of being born a heterosexual individual. This does not mean that I have the right to engage in adultery if things are not going well at home. As a Christian my standing orders are without qualification—no adultery. This principle holds true for those who have homosexual tendencies.

Some have become homosexual through experimentation or seduction. Other homosexual individuals are born with that pattern. This is a very real difficulty but can be made a special opportunity.

Two men I know whose work was very considerable for the Kingdom of God were born homosexuals. Both channelled their whole natures into God's way but homosexual activity had no part in their lives.

God's view of Sodom and its homosexuality are very clear. Read what he has to say: 'They gave up God: and therefore God gave them up— to be the playthings of their own foul desires in dishonouring their own bodies ... God therefore handed them over to disgraceful passions. Their women exchanged the normal practices of sexual intercourse for something which is abnormal and unnatural. Similarly the men, turning from natural intercourse with women, were swept into lustful passions for one another. Men with men performed these shameful horrors, receiving, of course, in their own personalities the consequences of sexual perversity' (Romans 1: 24, 26-27 Phillips).

These words should be read and reread. It is the sternest STOP, GO BACK, YOU'RE GOING THE WRONG WAY sign. God's pronouncement on perversion is that those who do these things deserve to die, though he is still prepared to forgive anyone who repents.

To sum it all up:

'God's plan is to make you holy, and that entails first of all a clean cut with sexual immorality.

'Every one of you should learn to control his body, keeping it pure and treating it with respect, and never regarding it as an instrument for self-gratification, as do pagans with no knowledge of God.

'You cannot break this rule without, in some way, cheating your fellow men. And you must remember that God will punish all who do offend in this matter, and we have warned you how we have seen this work out in our experience of life.

'The calling of God is not to impurity but to the most thorough purity, and anyone who makes light of the matter is not making light of a man's ruling but of God's command.

'It is not for nothing that the Spirit God gives us is called the *Holy* Spirit' (1 Thessalonians 4:3-8 Phillips).

21
HONEST TO GOD
Honesty

'It's gone,' said my African friend. 'My brand new watch. It was there on the ward table a minute ago. It cost me two months' wages.'

'There are only six people who could have stolen it, Daudi. I didn't. The two men with the broken legs couldn't. The old blind man had no idea it was even there, and that leaves the very thin, cunning boy with the bad chest and the tall, silent man who has great wisdom in breeding cattle.'

We went over to where these two were standing. Daudi told them what had happened. The cattle expert shook his head.

Juma, the boy with the cough, sneered. 'Why don't you do something about our sickness? Have I not got great pain in my chest where my hostile ancestors keep on stabbing me?'

I nodded. 'Well said, Juma. Let us see if we can do something more to help your troubles. Both of you take off your shirts and I will examine your chests.'

The tall man did so at once. Juma took a step backwards. 'I refuse.'

'Lift your arms above your heads.' The tall man grunted with pain but did so. Juma shook his head. 'I refuse.'

Daudi grinned. 'Then there is only one way left for us to help you, Juma. Come into the room where we keep the X-ray machine. We will examine your chest with that.'

'Was not this the reason that I came to hospital?' growled Juma.

The cattle expert raised one eyebrow and grinned as I listened to his chest with my stethoscope. Then we all went into the X-ray room.

The blinds were pulled down and as it became dark you could feel Juma's confidence growing.

'Keep your arms tightly by your side,' ordered Daudi, putting him in front of the X-ray and adjusting the fluorescent screen.

I put on a lead-lined apron and gloves and switched on the power. It was all a bit eerie. Juma drew his breath in sharply. As the odd green light appeared on the screen a confident half-smile was around his lips. I focused. You could see his heart beating. The bones of his chest and shoulders moved as he breathed; but the thing that stood out starkly black was the shadow of a wrist watch.

Daudi lifted a large mirror. Juma peered into it and his jaw dropped.

'Under your arm,' said Daudi quietly, 'is my watch. We can't see it with our ordinary eyes but X-rays bring to light the things that you can't see otherwise.'

Honesty is far more than not taking what isn't your own.

God says unmistakably NO STEALING. See Exodus 20, verse 15.

Two commandments further along he widens the matter when he says NO COVETING—a word not well understood but uncomfortably real in the lives of very many people. It is wanting something keenly that you don't have—wanting it in such a way that you bend all your energies to get it. You develop a burning greed for it and a willingness to manipulate anything by honest or dishonest means to get hold of it.

Honesty starts off in your mind and remains there while you refuse to be sidetracked from God's way.

Partial honesty does not meet God's requirements. And you do not need to be congratulated on honesty forced upon you by circumstances.

The same is true for the kind of honesty that only comes from lack of opportunity to be dishonest, or from fear of losing your reputation if you are found out.

Stealing is the obvious spot to start thinking in detail.

It's the fact of stealing that matters, not the amount that you steal. You may steal material things, money, goods—anything which attracts your attention.

You steal money when you're paid for time you don't work. The same thing is true if you take days off for sickness when you are not sick.

It is also only too possible for a boss to steal from those he employs.

You are stealing others' brains when you cheat in examinations, crib, copy homework or plagiarise.

You may steal a reputation by gossip, malicious talk, or even a shrug of the shoulders.

It is useless to try and justify your action by long explanations or rationalisation. It may smooth your conscience but it does nothing else.

The act of stealing is not made less by calling it a different name. You may pinch, scrounge, snitch, shoplift, or 'borrow' but the fact of theft is the same.

These are times when it is widely felt that there is a lack of honesty.

Maybe it is in government circles, and the thought is that the whole truth has not been told to the people.

Maybe it is the values of society that have been foisted on the unwilling. Maybe it is the 'do what I say, not what I do' approach.

But those who will wave banners in the cause of honesty in some areas will happily and with numb consciences be thoroughly dishonest in the matter of paying fares. The complaint is loud and clear if they are underpaid but solemn silence greets overpayment. These people fiddle their expense accounts and taxation returns. They hide much-sought-after books in odd corners in university libraries, or they take a liberal view in the use of the boss's time with personal e-mails and phone calls.

If you are honest before God you don't walk over the line that he has put down which reads NO STEALING.

In true Christian honesty, your mind is made up in the matter of theft. Shut the door of your mind to keep the whole idea intact and keep it shut and locked. The Holy Spirit will help keep you when temptation advises you to pick the lock. If your honesty-door is on the latch or easily opened, watch it. Given the circumstances and with a convenient patch of darkness, your hand flies into the till if you feel you can get away with it.

In the large department store there were hundreds of people who were examining goods under bright lights.

The shop detective was complacent. These were almost entirely genuine buyers apart from those two who were lingering in the CD department. He moved unobtrusively in their direction.

Suddenly all the lights went out. All of them.

There was some nervous laughter and many people streamed towards the street, stumbling and bumping into things. There was strange activity in the darkness of the great store. Four minutes later the lights came on again. In that short time thousands of dollars worth of goods were stolen—some by the few who were there to steal but the vast majority who shoplifted that day were 'honest' people and proud of the fact. They just took advantage of the darkness.

The opportunity came. They had no definite state of mind regarding stealing but, when given the chance and confronted with the prospect of not being seen or found out, they stole.

Honesty is one of the ways of seeing the change in the character of a person who has become one of God's family.

Incidentally, lying of any colour you care to nominate is rank dishonesty. And no liar has a place in the Kingdom of God (Revelation 21, verse 27).

22
PUNCTURED
'Small' Sins

Simba was a large, smiling African with the strength of a lion and a very great love for God and his way.

He and I were driving over a narrow road hacked through the jungle on our way to meet a high official. We had to be thirty miles away in two hours' time. Twenty miles an hour was good going over rough tracks and dry riverbeds, so we had allowed plenty of time for delays.

Abruptly the car skidded. '*Yoh!*' said Simba. 'A puncture.'

We climbed out of the old model Ford in time to see and hear a front tyre going flat. There were thorns all over the path. Iron-hard thorns as long as your little finger.

'Careful, Simba,' I urged. 'If those thorns get into your feet you will have no joy.'

'They have already pierced the feet of the machine, Bwana, and produced a matter of holdups and delay.'

Simba had no special use for jacks. He lifted the front of the car and I slipped a box under the axle. As we changed the wheel, again it came—the sound of escaping air. Simba sighed. 'Behold, there goes another one.'

This time we removed the tyre and found six thorns each of which had produced a puncture. We pulled these out with the aid of an outdated pair of dental forceps.

Simba marked the spots on the tube where the punctures were and I put patches in place. We hardly spoke a word. With the skill that came from long practice Simba slipped the tyre over the mended tube and reached for the pump.

I went to inspect the back wheels. One tyre was horribly flat. I grunted. Simba followed my gaze and raised his eyebrows.

My face went red with anger. Simba looked at me anxiously, but this did not stop my gush of words. 'Why can't the women cut the thorns off their firewood in the forest and not leave them here on the road to give us all this trouble?'

I was sweating hard, as I ran my hand through the grease and red dust in my hair. Simba nodded silently and lifted the back of the car. With a grunt I kicked the box into place. 'It's wretchedly hot and I'm a mess. How can I greet the great ones like this...?'

Again thorns were removed—a dozen of them—and patches duly put in place. My head throbbed. The sun was beating down. There was no shade. My African friend's voice came quietly. 'You wouldn't believe it but the other back tyre is...' He shrugged.

This was too much for me. My mouth was dry and my back ached. The sight of that fourth tyre squashing into the ground was the last straw.

'Why must we have a miserable old car that no one would use in Australia? Why is it that we can only get these rotten four-ply tyres? Why have we got to put up with all this?' I kicked the tool kit. 'I reckon we know every evil-minded thorn in the whole of this wretched jungle.'

Simba suddenly stood to his full height and his voice had a strong ring about it. 'Is that so, Bwana? Then what do you say is the name of this thorn?' He held up in the dental forceps a particularly vicious-looking specimen. I looked at him with my mouth open and said nothing. He looked me in the eye and said slowly, 'The name of this thorn is *grumbling*.' He pulled out another. It took some strong wrist work. 'This one *is bad temper*.'

I was speechless, but he went on, 'And this one—*resentment*, and this—*self-pity*,' Simba knew me uncomfortably well.

I had another of those odd experiences in which a spotlight seemed to come into my understanding. I grinned ruefully. 'You're so right, Simba. Your words have great value.'

We knelt beside that ancient machine and asked God to forgive us for the thorns that held up our progress for him. We asked him to help us avoid them in our travel as we moved on through life.

It was one of the most useful mornings I've ever lived. I stuck some of those thorns into a corn stalk. They weren't ornamental but they were a sharp reminder.

It was a crown of thorns that the soldiers forced down onto Jesus' forehead before they drove the spikes through his hands.

We, too, can wound him all over again with our particular thorns—these *smaller* sins of ours.

Look at what God says in Ephesians chapter 4, verse 30 to chapter 5, verse 4.

- No more resentment
- No more anger or temper
- No more violent self-assertiveness
- No more slander
- No more malicious remarks.
- No more immorality in any form.

- No itch to get your hands on what belongs to others.
- No nastiness, flippancy or silliness in your conversation, but a sense of all we owe to God.

Why not discard your personal puncture-producers?

23

KEEP THE ACID INSIDE THE BATTERY

Criticism

The letter read, 'Would you come and speak at our church? We're suffering at the moment from a lot of criticism and bitterness. It would help if you could outline the principle of the uselessness of this sort of thing.'

This posed a problem.

When Jesus had a situation like this before him, often he told a story. Nobody is frightened of a storyteller and most people appreciate a story, especially if you can catch the eye as well as the ear.

I arrived at the church with a parcel. It was skilfully and professionally wrapped. There seemed little chance of it not being a beer bottle. I walked into church, a Bible under one arm and this intriguing parcel under the other. Moving up the aisle I was aware of people who were singing lustily, suddenly stopping and a whispering taking the place of singing. I sat down and placed the parcel in a conspicuous place. When I stood up to speak the parcel went with me and again could be seen by everybody.

I went in boots and all. 'The question is, "What's in this bottle?"'

People leaned forward. Some smiled, others nodded. 'First remember that Jesus was interested in cruets and their contents.

'He talked about being the salt of the earth. He talked about mustard. There was a time when advertisers organised a big, eat-more-mustard drive. People wore badges; there were slogan competitions, crossword puzzles—a vast promotional gimmick to get people to use mustard. It had a tremendous effect, but in due course it faded out.

'Now I have come today to ask you to resign from another club.' Slowly I worked on the parcel. The congregation whispered and smiled. Wrapping after wrapping came off and then the label was in view. VINEGAR. A small sigh came from my listeners. I held the bottle above my head.

'The club I want you to resign from is the Vinegar Club. Membership can set your teeth on edge and do all manner of harm to other people and no good to anybody, especially yourself.

'Here is an acrostic to anchor it in your memory. You will find the whole matter drawn up at the end of the fourth chapter of Ephesians. I am using Phillips' translation as a basis:

V. *Vicious talk*. God particularly mentions violent self-assertiveness, slander and malicious remarks! "Be kind to one another; be understanding," God says.

I. *Impurity*. Paul covers sexual immorality in all its forms.

N. *Nastiness*. Find it in the last verse. The keynote of your conversation should not be nastiness or silliness or flippancy, but a sense of all that we owe to God.

E. *Envy* and its horrible twin, *jealousy*.

G. *Gossip, grousing, grumbling*.

A. *Anger*.

R. (the sourest of the lot) – *Resentment*.'

Forget the congregation. Forget the look on their faces and have a look at your own. Is it red?

There is no value in retaining membership in the Vinegar Club. It only means that you are playing life the enemy's way, you are achieving a minimum for your Lord and you are bringing no joy into your own living or that of anybody else.

What's the positive thing to do? Have a look at what are the fruits of the Spirit and build them into your living (Galatians 5:22-23).

While I have given up my subscription and membership in this particular club, I have a large number of 'vinegary' temptations which have the uncomfortable smell of acid about them. They will do no damage if you keep the bottle securely corked and safely locked in the back of the cupboard.

24
PAUSE FOR A WISH
Interlude

1. I wish I was rid of my ugly temper, spiteful tongue, and dirty mind.

    What stops you?

    You have God's diagnosis and cure. Do you admit to the diagnosis?

    What use are you making of his cure?

    To you it's free. It cost him more than we can ever realise.

2. I wish I could turn back the clock.

    You can't. But Jesus can deal completely with the past. He will take charge of your present and has pledged his word on your future.

3. I wish I was sure of everlasting life.

    You can be just that.

    Turn back to Chapter 5 for the answer.

4. I wish I could know where I'll be in five years' time.

    If you choose to go God's way, at any time in the future you'll be in the most strategic place.

5. I wish I could win the lottery.

    So you still have the idea that money is what really matters?

    Try putting your pocket into God's keeping and have another look at Chapter 15.

6. I wish those people who have done rotten things to me knew what it was like.

    They never will.

    They're built that way.

    But you can be sure that your Lord fully understands.

    Try praying for those people. That's positive action.

7. I wish I didn't have to read the Bible.

    Your wish is granted.

    There is no need at all—if you want your soul to be weak, your life to be fruitless and your joy and purpose to drain away.

8. I wish I could do exactly what I like.

    Of course you can.

    There's a useful Spanish proverb: 'Take what you like, says God, but pay for it.' God always forgives upon true confession and repentance, but your body doesn't.

25

TOW-ROPE
Fellowship

'If you run true to average,' I told the committee of a Christian student group, 'only three of you will be active for God seven years later.'

This so stirred them that they decided to pray for each other and to keep in regular touch so that through positive fellowship they might not drop out.

It worked. And now, fifteen years later, they are all on the job for God.

Fellowship is vital—praying together, working together, witnessing together, giving help and support when someone's feet start slipping or when someone comes up against problems and difficulties.

Alfred and Stanley were two cheerful young African friends of mine who loved God and cared for people. Their special work was comprehensive child welfare in Tanzania.

In the rainy season they would go out on safari, each in a separate Land Rover.

If they came to a place where the road turned into a black-soil bog, or if the normally dry rivers were running with muddy water, one man would get out and test the track on foot. If it seemed reasonable to try to cross, the first man would drive on. If he made it safely he would hitch his rope to the back axle of his Land Rover, walk back and attach the other end to the front axle of his friend's machine. Then, working together with considerable understanding, they would make the crossing a certainty.

The great fellowship verse is 1 John 1, verse 7: 'If we walk in the light, as he is in the light, we have fellowship with one another, and the blood of Jesus, his Son, purifies us from all sin.'

Walking in the light we can see one another. We have the path under view. We can help one another.

Fellowship by post and phone are very practical. A letter from time to time to your Christian friends. A letter of encouragement. A letter to bring comfort. An e-mail asking for help. When I was in deep trouble I sent a cable from East Africa, 'What's wrong with your knees?'

Fellowship is the antidote to backsliding. There is neither joy nor purpose in backsliding.

There is fellowship in your church. You can give it as well as receive it. Worship is of high importance.

Have a look at Hebrews 10, verses 24 and 25. Phillips translates it, 'Let us think of one another and how we can encourage one another to love and do good deeds.

'And let us not hold aloof from our church meetings, as some do.

'Let us do all we can to help one another's faith, and this the more earnestly as we see the final day drawing ever nearer.'

26
A MATTER OF LIFE AND DEATH
Death

Some of you who read this are certain to die in a car accident if we are to believe statistics. Cancer will account for others, heart disease for still more . . . and so it goes on. These are the facts of death.

George Bernard Shaw said, 'The statistics of death are quite impressive. One out of one people die.'

When you hear an ambulance there is the fleeting feeling of, 'Poor chap, I hope he gets on all right,' and then you're thinking of something else.

It's different when *you* are in the ambulance.

'Would you like oxygen, doctor?' asked the ambulance man who was putting the stretcher with me on it into the vehicle.

Smoothly I was taken to hospital and soon lay in bed panting. I felt that my ribs were tied tightly with a mass of cords. Breathing was a battle and it seemed

I was losing that battle. Asthma can be a far from friendly complaint.

Later I lay in bed propped up on pillows. A drip was in my arm and an oxygen mask over my nose. The only exercise I could manage was thinking.

As a small boy I had been given a scrap of paper with a couplet typed on it:

'When I am dying how glad I shall be
That the lamp of my life has been blazed out for Thee.'

I hated those words then because I wanted life and didn't want even to think of death. But as I lay in the hospital I was excited to think that there was a fair chance of my setting out on the most splendid safari of the lot. I thought how good it was to know that my name was written in 'the Lamb's book of life' (Revelation 21:27).

There are three sorts of death.

Physical death—when your soul is separated from your body. This is the ordinary death you see recorded in obituary columns.

Spiritual death—when your soul is separated from God. Sin is the wall that divides. Millions are walking round in this state. There is absolutely no need for them to keep on doing so.

Eternal death—when body and soul are separated from God forever. This doesn't mean the cessation of existence. It is what happens when physical death is added to spiritual death.

How does this apply to individuals?

Take me for instance. What is true for me, of course, applies to everyone who has become a Christian.

I can undergo physical death. My soul will be separated from my body. There will be a funeral—all the routine. But I won't experience spiritual death because I am united with my Lord. The wall of sin has been broken down. Jesus did this for me.

I won't undergo eternal death: 'Whoever believes in him shall not perish but have eternal life.' (John 3:16) But if I turn my back on God and persist in living that way, eternal death is inevitable.

As far as my spiritual death was concerned—yes, I was spiritually dead in trespasses and sins. But God, when I asked him, made me alive in Christ.

Sometimes death can be very close to birth.

One African afternoon, driving through a village, Daudi and I heard the wailing sound which tells of death.

We were quickly on the spot. A child had been born—the fifth child to this mother and, like the other four, it had been born dead, or so they told us. Quickly I looked at the baby lying on an old piece of blanket.

My stethoscope told me the heart was still beating but the baby was not breathing. A child may survive quite a number of minutes after birth without breathing and this child was potentially alive. However, something was stopping his lungs from opening out like a parachute and breathing.

This was vital for him to become physically alive.

We worked at a great rate.

'It's useless,' said the old women. The mother wept hopelessly.

Daudi and I dramatically produced a plug of rubbish as big as my thumb from the child's throat. Filthy, clogging, dark mucus.

'He is dead,' said the old women.

'My child, my child,' wailed the mother. 'He's dead.'

'*Waah!*' said the baby.

From looking like an armful of wet socks, he changed in a matter of seconds to a living, breathing boy baby.

The thing that mattered was getting that plug of muck out of his airway and letting his lungs do their normal job. If the obstruction had stayed in the windpipe, the baby would have been dead. His heart was beating. He was potentially alive but in a matter of minutes he would have been another dead infant— stillborn, instead of lying alive and normal in his delighted mother's arms.

LIFE AFTER BIRTH

Look at the various sorts of birth:

Physical birth: When you are physically born, you are only potentially alive. Your heart is beating but, unless you breathe, you have never actually lived. If the airway to your lung is blocked you do not begin to live. If the blockage is removed, you live. That blockage is an excellent picture of sin.

Spiritual birth: People who are physically alive are not automatically spiritually alive. Jesus said they must experience a second birth—a spiritual one.

As a newly-born infant cannot remove an obstruction from his throat, no more can a person remove the obstruction of sin by themselves from their soul.

Jesus is completely able to do this for us and will if asked. A person is thus born again. Jesus becomes Saviour and Lord and the individual becomes a new creature going God's way. His soul is alive.

'As members of a sinful race all men die; as members of the Christ of God all men shall be raised to life … all who belong to him' (1 Corinthians 15:22-23 Phillips).

27
SHARE MY GOOD NEWS
Witness

The African chief was fighting for breath. Ten minutes before I had been doing the same.

His bloodshot eyes were fixed on me and he panted. 'Give me some of it. It's a medicine of strength. It works.'

'Perhaps it won't work for you. Great One. Perhaps it will damage you. Perhaps...'

The chief staggered to his feet. 'Give it to me. You have the same trouble as I have. You took that medicine. I've seen it work for you. I want it now.'

He was given the same medicine in the same dose. Scores of his people crowded round. Sometimes ten minutes can go very slowly. It certainly did that scorching, windy, East African day.

As minute followed minute and nothing seemed to be happening, hostility grew. Angry murmurs became louder until suddenly the tall man's face burst into a wide smile. 'It works. I breathe. The tight bonds that tied my ribs together come undone. It's a medicine of strength, truly.'

'This medicine has helped us both. We had the same trouble and the same remedy helped each of us.'

'It is a thing of joy,' he agreed, taking deep breaths.

The sharing of the medicine that gave me the upper hand with asthma gained me a friend and gave me a tailor-made chance of telling him about the Lord Jesus Christ.

As useful a title as any for this sort of activity is *witnessing*.

If you have become a Christian, whoever you are and wherever you are, you have a special piece of good news to pass on.

As you come alongside people, they have the opportunity of seeing Jesus in your life while you have the chance to tell them about him.

School and university are among the best places. Over 70 percent of people who become Christians do so during their childhood and student days. The witness of young person to young person is ideal and most effective.

One of the last things that Jesus said on earth was that we were to be witnesses to him at home, in our district, in our country, and to have a world outreach. This instruction applies to everyone in his family. Jesus' actual words are in Acts 1, verse 8.

God is more concerned about people than we are. We can therefore be sure that if we are willing to tell others about him and if we pray for opportunities— opportunities will present themselves.

There are many useful methods of sharing Christ with others. By all means use them. But don't be tied down by them.

Christian books are very handy. Lend them. Don't give them away in the first instance. This supplies you with the opportunity of talking about the book's contents when it is brought back.

Inviting someone to church and following up the matter at home or on the way home is a tried, helpful approach.

But nothing takes the place of personal friendship and careful thought and prayer which leads to fruitful conversation.

Your responsibility is not met by pushing a booklet into a letterbox after dark or leaving a tract in the train.

Being quietly on hand in an emergency may give the chance you've been praying for. Illness and catastrophe often make people aware of larger issues.

Starting into a conversation about God needs to be carefully done.

A doctor, trying to help a very sick person, asked gently, 'Have you any religious convictions?'

One of the patient's eyes opened and a whisper came back reproachfully, 'I've never been in jail in my life.'

Use language that will be understood and have a copy of the Bible readily available. You will need to refer to it.

There is value in getting people to read things for themselves.

Watch your life and your living. Christians must be prepared to live behind glass.

'You are the world's light—it is impossible to hide a town built on the top of a hill. Men do not light a lamp and put it under a bucket. They put it on a lamp-stand and it gives light for everybody in the house.

'Let your light shine like that in the sight of men. Let them see the good things you do and praise your Father in heaven' (Matthew 5:14-16 Phillips).

28
SALT
Witness without Savour

They stood around talking in the shade of the University buildings. Mild surprise was their reaction to the questions the guest speaker had asked about what steps they, as Christian students, took to pass on the good news to others on campus and at large.

A louder voice came out with, 'After all we're here to think, to discuss, to weigh up, to evaluate.' This was greeted with nods and varied sounds of agreement.

I had listened to the guest speaker. His practical thinking and enthusiasm for action seemed hardly to have touched his listeners.

Later the Student President approached me. 'We're having a weekend discussion on the theology of evangelism. There will be seminars and workshops. It should be great. We would want you to give the first talk.'

I nodded. The alert young man went on. 'If you could give us an appetiser, soup before the main meal idea.'

'I'll be glad to do that. By the way have you seen any result from your witness so far this year?'

'We've only been going for five months.'

'If you've planted and cultivated, you should be having some result by now. Remember John 15, verse 16.'

He smiled and nodded vaguely, so I quoted: 'You did not choose me, but I chose you and appointed you to go and bear fruit – fruit that will last.'

He rapidly retreated and the thought came, 'Maybe I'd make more impact by aiming for the hide rather than the head.'

Schemes of various sorts and subtlety were considered and then the answer came one day in a supermarket as I bought a packet of powdered gelatin.

I drove early to the conference centre and headed for the kitchen. The cook was an active Christian. His excellent cooking backed up his cheerful, friendly approach to people.

'Doc,' he said, 'this lot don't seem interested in spreading the Good News; they seem to be trying to hatch it. Any suggestions?'

I grinned, 'John, here is a packet of powdered gelatin. Let me help you to plan the menu. It's cold; can you turn on soup and stew?'

He nodded, 'Easy, what's in your mind?'

'Between us we'll preach a sermon they'll find hard to forget.' We chatted and chuckled and then prayed that our plan would be seen as a useful thing and no mere practical joke.

I spent an hour filling saltshakers with powdered gelatin while he dealt with vegetables like a juggler.

At sundown John had cauldrons simmering in a way to delight the nose.

Dinner time arrived and with it a hungry, chilly horde who flooded the room.

Steaming soup came in large plates. Spoons went into action and then it started.

'*Ugh!* No salt! Pass the salt.'

Disgruntled voice, 'Tasteless stuff. *Yuk!*"

Academic voice, 'Isn't the soup unappetising and unsavoury?'

Grumbling rumbled round the dining room. The volume increased when the stew arrived looking and smelling everything a stew should, but saltless. Every saltshaker produced its cascade of white powder. Then someone tasted that same white powder.

There was an outcry. They shouted for the cook. They counted him out and demanded salt—the real thing. He produced the box labelled SALT. Sampling showed it was tasteless. Voices were raised.

'Rotten grocer.'

'Rotten cook. We ought to drown him in it.'

'It's some rotten practical joker.'

The academic voice, unnaturally shrill, 'I don't think I shall come here again.'

A distinctly disgruntled group sat round a large log fire to hear what I had to say.

I started, 'Active Christians often find themselves in the soup. The right place for salt, as you possibly will remember, is in the soup.'

This was greeted by a chorus of groans and a little laughter.

I held up my hand. There were punches in my voice. 'You made it obvious what you thought of your soup and your stew. Please understand clearly that *I* planned your unsatisfactory meal. *I* bought that gelatin. *I* filled the shakers with phony salt. Your palates are still insulted by the flavourless food you've eaten. The only way to force a point into some people's memories and their sense of responsibility is not via their minds but via their stomachs.'

There was dead silence while I paused—a lengthy pause, 'Your witness has been just this. You've had a tasteless, resultless year so far. A harvest of bushels of words.

'Tasteless salt is useless salt. Have a look at Matthew 5, verse 13.

'Powdered gelatin looks the part but it doesn't do the job.

'There is no purpose or joy in being insipid witnesses to your Lord Jesus Christ. He expects fruit and fruit that endures.

'The choice before you is to carry on smugly and ineffectively, or humbly to go out for results for him.'

Again I paused. 'Now what about spending two minutes in silent prayer.'

When those two minutes were over I was a kilometre away on my way home and having a close look at the saltiness of my own witness at home, in hospital and at large.

29
LIVING BEHIND GLASS
Christian Behaviour

The lights changed at the pedestrian crossing. An engine roared and a car shot past on the wrong side, weaving through the traffic and pulling up with a screech of brakes. Any traffic cop would have issued a ticket for dangerous driving.

When we, too, stopped at the red light we were interested to note that the back of the car was liberally decorated with slogans like *Jesus is the real thing* and *Smile, God loves you*. The lights had barely changed to green when, with a loud complaint from the tyres, the car rocketed on.

I thought, 'I hope that's a stolen car. If it isn't, it would be much better if they removed those slogans. The people driving that car are only making a laughing-stock of the One they say they serve.'

Throughout this book there has been mention of the believing side and the behaving side of your life.

The first is your way of entering God's family and growing in it.

The behaving phase is utterly different. It's the shop window of your life. If you have let Jesus take charge, your life will show it by what you do and how you do it. It's no good saying that Jesus will change your life if obviously your life is not changed.

Think of the things that may not mean a snap of the fingers to you but to others matter a lot.

Crankiness: By all means get out of the wrong side of the bed and take it out on the ones you care for most. Use the rough side of your tongue. It's your right if you want it that way.

A smiling face is so much better than a scowling one. You can hear a smile in the voice. There's a delightful synthetic proverb which reads: No smile, no serve in shop.

Consideration of others: There's the character that blows in for a meal, spends the evening giving a full list of all his woes and complaints and then toots his horn in farewell. It sounds better after midnight. He also has a slogan on the back window of his car reading: 'Honk if you love Jesus.'

Punctuality: 'But I don't even have a watch. Time means nothing to me.' But it does to most people who also need sleep.

He rings up at all hours.

He stamps in late and his shoes creak. It's tough on the speaker, the listeners lose concentration. It wakens the baby.

'Thank you' is easy to pronounce and it's music to the ears of the one who worked hard to produce an appetising meal.

Of course there is no need to say it. Your right is to do as you like. This is freedom. But if Jesus is your Lord, your behaviour pattern will follow his.

Luke 6, verse 40 says, 'A disciple is not above his teacher, but when he is fully trained he will be like his teacher' (Phillips).

The standard of our behaviour is the way Jesus behaved and the guideline is set down clearly in God's word. Our objective is full training.

In conversation at a university I asked, 'Do you ever talk to people about Jesus?'

The student shook his head. 'I used to try but they didn't listen.' The facts were he knew his life often did not back up his words. He tried too little and gave up too early.

Watch that your everyday dealings with people don't put the lie to the things you profess.

30

FOR HEAVEN'S SAKE
Christian Zeal

One African morning we went into the outpatients' room for staff prayers. The floor was of polished cement. You could almost see your face in it.

Everyone was sitting quietly when in came a small boy, dressed in very little. He looked owlishly at people and was suddenly violently sick on the polished floor.

'*Mmmfp*,' I said. 'Let's go outside.'

But Daudi was on his feet. 'Doctor. Please let me speak this morning, and in here.'

'But Daudi...'

He looked at me. 'I have something to say. I think it is from God.'

What he said I will never forget. For the way he said it nailed it up in my mind, and I hope the same happens to you.

Daudi looked at that unlovely pool on the floor and asked, 'What is the value of vomit?'

I saw noses wrinkle and people draw back.

'*Mmff!*' sniffed someone.

Daudi went on. 'How much would you pay for a pint of vomit?'

'*Ukk!*' gulped a nurse. 'Oh, no!'

There was a gleam in Daudi's eye. 'You do not like it? Truly it is not food for the eyes nor yet food for the nose. Also it brings no music to the ears. Vomit is a thing of no beauty and of no joy.'

I interrupted him. 'Daudi, listen. What's all this about?'

He gave me a little smile. 'Hear my words. In the last book of the Bible, third chapter, it is written, 'Because you are neither cold nor hot I will vomit you out of my mouth.' God has no joy, not even a little, in people who are neither cold nor hot.' He pointed to the floor. 'Is that what God seeks when he looks at you?'

And you. When it comes to the matter of the Kingdom of God, are you merely lukewarm?

Try some zeal.

Feel the touch of urgency.

What about some wholehearted faith and some complete obedience? Keep directly on the target (and no red herrings, whether they smell holy or not).

A challenge was put to me when I was a student: 'Ask God to give you the willingness, knowledge and help to win at least one soul a year for his kingdom. It's your responsibility then to help him or her to grow in Christian faith, knowledge and witness.'

To me achieving this has been one of life's adventures and greatest happinesses.

When you reach the autumn of your life you will be more than thankful that you used the spring wisely.

'Never be lacking in zeal, but keep your spiritual fervour, serving the Lord' (Romans 12:11).

JUNGLE DOCTOR HOSPITAL SERIES

JUNGLE DOCTOR ANIMAL STORIES

Jungle Doctor's Fables
There was once a monkey who didn't believe in crocodiles.
ISBN: 978-1-84550-608-7

Jungle Doctor's Monkey Tales
Small monkeys never could remember not to get too near to the hind fee of zebra.
ISBN: 978-1-84550-609-4

Jungle Doctor's Tug-of-War
Even by monkey standards, Toto was pretty dim. The Jungle underworld think he will turn out to be easy meat.
ISBN: 978-1-84550-610-0

Jungle Doctor's Hippo Happenings
Boohoo the Unhappy Hippo had a great deal of empty space between his strangely-shaped ears.
ISBN: 978-1-84550-611-7

Jungle Doctor's Rhino Rumblings
Rhino has small eyes, a big body, a tiny brain, and a huge idea of his own importance.
ISBN: 978-1-84550-612-4

Jungle Doctor meets Mongoose
Again and again the snake struck, but the flying ball of fur with the fiery eyes always managed to jump backwards.
ISBN: 978-1-84550-613-1

CHRISTIAN FOCUS PUBLICATIONS

Christian Focus | Christian Heritage | CF4K | Mentor

Christian Focus Publications publishes books for adults and children under its four main imprints: Christian Focus, CF4K, Mentor and Christian Heritage. Our books reflect that God's word is reliable and Jesus is the way to know him, and live for ever with him.

Our children's publication list includes a Sunday School curriculum that covers pre-school to early teens; puzzle and activity books. We also publish personal and family devotional titles, biographies and inspirational stories that children will love.

If you are looking for quality Bible teaching for children then we have an excellent range of Bible story and age specific theological books.

From pre-school to teenage fiction, we have it covered!

Find us at our web page:
www.christianfocus.com

CF4•K
Because you're never too young to know Jesus